Journeys Into Matthew

Journeys Into Matthew

18 Lessons of Exploration and Discovery

Raymond Apicella

St. Anthony Messenger Press
Cincinnati, Ohio

Nihil Obstat: Rev. Nicholas Lohkamp, O.F.M.
Rev. Robert L. Hagedorn

Imprimi Potest: Rev. John Bok, O.F.M.
Provincial

Imprimatur: +Carl K. Moeddel, V.G.
Archdiocese of Cincinnati
February 5, 1996

The *nihil obstat* and *imprimatur* are a declaration that a book
is considered to be free from doctrinal or moral error. It is not
implied that those who have granted the *nihil obstat* and *imprimatur* agree with the contents, opinions or statements
expressed.

Cover and book design by Julie Lonneman

ISBN 0-86716-183-3

Published by St. Anthony Messenger Press
Printed in the U.S.A.

Acknowledgments

I have been able to complete this manual only because of the
extraordinary assistance and bountiful kindness offered me
during the research and writing. I am deeply grateful to Lisa
Biedenbach, managing editor of St. Anthony Messenger Press,
for her understanding and patience throughout the project.
Thanks are due to the faculty and staff of the Institute for
Pastoral Ministries of St. Thomas University for their constant
encouragement. Support and service were also offered to me
by the dedicated library staff of St. Thomas University through
their willingness to assist in the researching of biblical material. I am especially thankful to my friends Roger Allee, Patty
DiEgido, Bonny and Stu Larson and Pat Green for their gentle
prodding and encouragement to finish the manual. Deserving
of my deepest appreciation is my wife, Elizabeth Jackson, who
not only supported me along the way but patiently and lovingly
critiqued my writing.

Dedication

To the Brothers of Holy Cross—especially of the Eastern and
Southern Provinces—for their spiritual training and academic
opportunities.

Contents

Introduction

Journeys Into Matthew is a companion to *Journeys Into Mark* and *Journeys Into Luke*. Designed for the adult learner, it derives from the undergraduate, graduate and adult continuing education Scripture courses I teach at St. Thomas University, Miami, Florida, and parishes of the Archdiocese of Miami. These teaching and learning experiences have convinced me that it is essential to combine theoretical material with an application to the life of the community if we are to understand the Scriptures. Each Journey is offered not as mere factual material unrelated to personal life, but as a way for readers to develop their intellectual and spiritual lives. The manual's two major components, background information and reflective exercises, are equally important when working with the exercises.

Journeys Into Matthew is presented in manual form. You are invited to record initial impressions, ideas and insights as the beginning of the learning experience. The responses become the basis for understanding within a particular Journey. Each exercise is designed to offer background information (Exploring), reflective exercises (Discovering), points of review (Looking Back) and a list of resources for future study (Exploring Further). Presented in a self-paced design, the exercises invite you to spend as much time as you need with any one Journey. All the exercises can be used by individuals and small groups.

Before You Journey

Scholars agree that we know less about the Gospel writers than we know about the Gospels themselves. None of the writers (including Matthew) place their names or personal vitae within the Gospel itself. Through a process of investigation scholars offer intelligent assumptions based on hints within the work or other reliable sources. Matthew's writing is dated somewhere between the years 80 to 90 C.E. (Common Era); many scholars select 85 C.E. as the most likely date.

Scholars refer to the writings of Matthew, Mark and Luke as Synoptic Gospels, that is, they can be viewed together with one (*syn*) look (*optic*). A popular theory held by many scholars is that Matthew and Luke followed the general outline of Mark's Gospel. Scholars also believe that both Matthew and Luke incorporated material from other sources. A major source used by Luke and Matthew is referred to as the "Q" source (from *quelle*, the German word for source), a hypothetical collection of sayings of Jesus. The "Q" source theory was presented by the German scholar C. H. Weiss in 1838. The theory that Matthew borrowed from Mark and "Q" will be discussed in greater detail within the Journeys.

Scholars do not believe that Matthew the author of the Gospel and Matthew the apostle are the same individual. Early Church theories postulated the writer Matthew as possibly a disciple of the apostle, who thereby received his information from an "official" eyewitness. More recent studies, however, provide an opposite point of view. If Matthew the writer were either the apostle or a disciple of the apostle, why does his Gospel depend heavily on at least two other sources, Mark and "Q," and not on more primary sources? Approximately 70 percent of Mark's Gospel is contained in Matthew's Gospel. If Matthew the apostle were the Gospel writer, why did he write in Greek and not Hebrew? A study of Matthew 24:15 refers to Daniel as a prophet, a reference only made in the Greek translation of the Old Testament. These are two examples of the kinds of questions scholars have asked. They show the breadth and depth of scholarly exploration of the Scriptures.

It is important to understand that the Church has never emphatically stated that the faithful must believe that a certain individual is the author of a particular Gospel. Rather in faith and through the teachings of the Church the Christian believes that the Gospels are inspired by God and reveal a way of salvation. For now, we can say that this Gospel is associated with a person named Matthew.

Comprehensive study of Matthew's Gospel suggests that his community may have come from Palestine and eventually settled in Syria. The community has strong Jewish roots as demonstrated by its reverence for Jewish Law and customs and its reference to Gentiles (non-Jews) as outsiders. The place (Syria) and the time (between 80 and 90 C.E.) is significant. At this time many believers still had roots in Judaism but they were beginning to separate from the beliefs of their ancestors. Prior to the Jewish revolt of the late 60's the early believers experienced a warm relationship with their Jewish brothers and sisters. This is documented in Acts 2, which says Jesus' followers continued to go to the Temple as part of their communal life. During the height of the Jewish revolt, when the Roman general

Titus destroyed Jerusalem and razed the Temple (around 70 C.E.), the relationships between Jews and Christians changed dramatically.

The destruction of the Temple significantly changed the religious practices of the Jews. It also had a profound impact on early groups of Christians who were forced to move their center from Jerusalem. For Matthew's community it is a time of great confusion and pain as they witness a breakdown in their relationship with their past and a need to launch into a new understanding of themselves as people of God and followers of the Messiah.

Matthew, like all the Gospel writers, reveals who God is by telling his readers who Jesus is. He emphasizes that Jesus is the fulfillment of Old Testament Law by structuring Jesus' ministry into five sermons, mirroring the five books of the Torah or Pentateuch (the first five books of our Old Testament). Throughout his Gospel Matthew demonstrates to his readers that the authority, teaching and presence of God are found in Jesus, the Christ.

Journey 1
Images of God

Several years ago the popular cartoon *Dennis the Menace* depicted Dennis sitting at an easel displaying his rendition of what God looks like. Although warned by his mother that no one knows what God looks like, Dennis, admiring his artistic drawing, boldly proclaims, "They do now!"

Although we may not have Dennis' confidence that we can depict adequately the "true image" of God, everyone has some image of God. The image may change with situations or remain constant. It may be something one takes for granted without time for reflection, or it may be so integral to one's religious heritage that it comes to mind frequently.

Discovering

In presenting Scripture lessons to people of all ages, I often begin by asking them to draw an image of God. Supplied with white paper and crayons, the artists are free to offer personal expressions of what God looks like. Reassured that there are no right or wrong images and that no one needs to be a Michelangelo, students through the years have produced a massive collection of images of God.

In the space provided draw your image of "what God looks like."

Exploring

Your image may fit one of the following categories common to drawings provided by other students. The images often depict God in a human manner (anthropomorphism), as a visible manifestation in nature (theophany), or as a combination of shapes and colors (transcendence). Some students leave the paper blank, another example of transcendent imaging.

These four types of artistic renditions are similar to the images of God presented in written form in the Old Testament. Read the following Scripture passages:

Genesis 3:8-24; *
1 Kings 19:9-13;
Isaiah 40:18.

The depiction in Genesis 3 is a God who moves about in the garden like a human being. The God depicted in 1 Kings is presented as a tiny whisper or a gentle breeze. Yet another image is presented in Isaiah where the prophet asks, "To whom can you liken God? With what equal can you confront him?"

No one biblical image of God totally captures what God is like, yet each image presents a brief glimpse of God. Likewise no one biblical account depicts totally what God is like. Rather the Bible is a collection of accounts that together begin to unfold for the reader what God is like. In the New Testament, the accounts about Jesus reveal a special depiction of what God is like. The New Testament reader comes to know what God is like by coming to know what Jesus is like.

Matthew's intent is to present an image of Jesus that will communicate an image of God to Greek-speaking Jewish Christians living during a period of intense hostility between Jews and Christians. The hostility has been mounting since the destruction of the Jewish Temple in Jerusalem around 70 C.E. (Common Era). Previous to this time Jewish Christians felt free to maintain Jewish practices and relationships. After the destruction of the Temple, the rabbis expelled all believers who were not followers of pure Mosaic Law claiming that they were abusing the Law and forfeiting their claim as the chosen people. Matthew argues that Christian believers are not forfeiting their claim to be among the chosen people because all Old Testament prophesies are fulfilled in Jesus. Thus he presents Jesus as one who has interpreted the principles of the higher law of love.

---

* In Gospel citations the first number refers to the chapter; this number is followed by a colon and the next number(s) indicate the verse(s). For example, Genesis 3:8-24 refers to the third chapter, verses 8-24, of the Book of Genesis. A long dash separating two numbers indicates that the passage covers more than one chapter, for example Genesis 1:1—2:4 refers to chapter one, verse one, through chapter two, verse four.

Discovering

The image of Jesus interpreting the higher law of love is presented throughout Matthew's Gospel. Ideally you should read the Gospel in one sitting, but that luxury may not be suitable for everyone's schedule. It is, however, essential to read the entire Gospel. For convenience you might divide it into the seven segments listed here. After reading each segment, write a line or two that briefly summarize the major points you discovered.

Read Matthew's Gospel:

1) Chapters 1—2

2) Chapters 3—7

3) Chapters 8—10

4) Chapters 11—13

5) Chapters 14—18

6) Chapters 19—25

7) Chapters 26—28

Exploring

Compare your summaries for each of the sections with mine.

- Chapters 1—2: stories of the birth of Jesus
- Chapters 3—7: how one is to live the Christian life (Beatitudes)
- Chapters 8—10: what it means to be a follower (disciple) of Jesus
- Chapters 11—13: parables on the Kingdom
- Chapters 14—18: what it means to be Church
- Chapters 19—25: stories about the endtime
- Chapters 26—28: the passion, death and resurrection of Jesus and the commissioning of the followers.

The loose division of Matthew's Gospel presented in the previous exercise hints at a more detailed division that many scholars have held for a long time. The division is one that I learned as a student of Neil Flanagan, O.F.M., while studying at the School of Applied Theology, Berkeley. This division provides us with a mechanism for quickly identifying sections of Matthew's Gospel. The Gospel has a formal beginning (birth stories) and a formal ending (passion, death, resurrection and commissioning). In between we have five sermons: Christian life, discipleship, parables, Church and endtime.

Discovering

In the space provided write the verse for each of the following citations.

Matthew 7:28

Matthew 11:1

Matthew 13:53

Matthew 19:1

Matthew 26:1

- Matthew 19:1: "When Jesus finished these words, he left Galilee and went to the district of Judea across the Jordan."

- Matthew 26:1: "When Jesus finished all these words, he said to his disciples,..."

Each verse reveals that Jesus has finished and is moving on. These words provide a verbal closure to the end of a section, thus separating Matthew's work into five major parts. Each part (or sermon) consists of an introduction and the sermon itself. A major portion of this manual will investigate Matthew's sermons.

Looking Back

On Journey 1 you made the following discoveries:

- The Old Testament presents images of God; in the New Testament Jesus reveals what God is like.
- Matthew presents his image of Jesus to a community struggling during great crisis.
- Matthew presents his image of Jesus in five sermons.

Exploring Further

Flanagan, Neil. *Mark, Matthew and Luke: A Guide to the Gospel Parallels.* Collegeville, Minn.: The Liturgical Press, 1978.

Exploring

Compare your verses with these from the *New American Bible With Revised New Testament.*

- Matthew 7:28: "When Jesus finished these words, the crowds were astonished at his teaching,..."

- Matthew 11:1: "When Jesus finished giving these commands to his twelve disciples, he went away from that place to teach and to preach in their towns."

- Matthew 13:53: "When Jesus finished these parables, he went away from there."

Journey 2
Tools of the Trade

In order to begin a journey into the Gospel of Matthew we need to gather some tools to help us on the way. The first thing we need to know is that the accounts presented in the Gospel began at a time when oral communication was more important than written. Some scholars believe that these stories were first sung. The rhythm of singing aids the memorization process. For example, children learning their ABC's often sing them.

We refer to the earliest accounts as the "oral tradition," stories whose major purpose was primarily to reveal that Jesus is the Christ. Gradually, as the community began to fear losing the story, individuals began to put the story in written form.

We also need to know that the Gospels are faith stories that relate an experience of God. The intent is not to present a biographical sketch of Jesus of Nazareth or an historical treatise of first-century Palestine, but rather to enable the person hearing the story to proclaim faithfully that Jesus is the Christ. The early Church expected the faithful to hear the message and respond with joy, "Maranatha! Come, Lord Jesus."

Finally, we need to realize that these are key stories, not exhaustive accounts. Stories capture the major events of our lives. We do not tell all the stories, only those that have had an impact on our lives. The stories we tell usually revolve around what we refer to as "aha" moments—those times in our lives when we come to a deeper understanding of the meaning of life. In Gospel terms, the writer presents those "aha" stories about Jesus that assist the hearer's faith.

As you journey through Matthew's Gospel, try to *hear* the story as if for the first time. You may need to train your ear in order to capture all the meaning found within the story.

Exploring

Some background into the Old Testament is needed in order to *hear* Matthew's story of Jesus. The short sketch of the religious history of the Israelite people presented in the following section doesn't do justice to the rich background needed to appreciate fully Matthew's Gospel. It is presented as a mere beginning, a glimpse of the relationships between major events in Matthew's Gospel and important Old Testament passages.

The Old Testament is the story of the relationship between God and the chosen people. It traces the development of a people from a motley crew of nomads brought together under a belief in one God, Yahweh, to a unified nation and mighty kingdom.

In the beginning, these people fell into slavery to Pharaoh only to be liberated by God through Moses' leadership. This great liberation event is the heart of the Israelites' story and is celebrated in the feast of Passover. Closely linked to the liberation event (the Exodus) is the Sinai event in which God gives Moses and the people a great covenant. The covenant (known as the Ten Commandments) is the guidepost for living life to the fullest. Once freed from the horrors of slavery and brought to the promised land, the Israelites flourish and become a kingdom under the great leadership of such kings as David. It is during the time when the Israelites are a mighty nation that they build a magnificent temple.

But destruction and tragedy afflict the people of God and outside forces begin to dominate the land. Destruction by the Babylonians brought about the razing of the first Temple and the great diaspora of the Jewish people. Later conquerors allowed the Jews to return and rebuild the Temple. (The second Temple is the Temple in existence during the historical time of Jesus and the one destroyed by the Romans around 70 C.E.)

During this time of destruction and civil strife the great prophets rise up to accuse the Israelites of their infidelity to God. Each time, the prophet tries to remind the Israelite people of the covenant given to them by God through Moses on Mt. Sinai.

Alongside the Law and the prophetic tradition is the wisdom material. It attests to the fact that human life was unthinkable without Yahweh. The teachers of wisdom instruct the people about discipline, moderation and hard work through the use of practical illustrations. Within the wisdom material people are called to "fear" the Lord—an obedience to the will of God with a profound sense of awe.

Discovering

Matthew is writing to a community aware of its Jewish roots. His Jewish-Christian community may have been struggling with the problem of being expelled from the synagogues while attempting to be faithful to both

Jewish Law and the Christian belief that Jesus is the Messiah.

The coming of the Messiah is a recurrent theme in the Old Testament. Matthew's Gospel demonstrates to early believers (whether from Jewish or Gentile backgrounds) how Jesus fulfills the Old Testament sayings about the coming Messiah. Matthew assumes that his readers know the message of the Hebrew Scriptures, an assumption that may be presumptuous when applied to today's students of the Gospel. Therefore we need to explain some of Matthew's references.

Read Matthew 1:17.
Read Matthew 1:12-16.

Summarize in a phrase or sentence the main concept expressed in Matthew 1:17 only.

Exploring

You may have noticed that Matthew 1:17 places the generations leading to Jesus in three groups of fourteen. However, if you refer to Matthew 1:12-16 and count the list of names associated with the period after the Babylonian exile, you notice that only thirteen names are listed. The miscounting appears to be deliberate on Matthew's part in order to make a theological point.

Numerology played an important part in the life of the Hebrew people. They believed that God uses numbers for both design and significance, for example, resting on the *seventh* day. In the New Testament the twelve apostles are parallel to the twelve tribes of Israel. Names were also given numerical value, which is significant for understanding Matthew 1:17. The number *fourteen* can be linked to the name David, Israel's greatest king. Because the Hebrew language contains no vowels, David becomes DVD. D has a numerical value of four, V has a value of six, so 4+6+4=14. Matthew intentionally groups the generations into periods of fourteen so that the "hearer" associates the number with David. This emphasizes that Jesus comes from the line of David, yet another Old Testament prophecy fulfilled.

In Journey 1 we suggested that Matthew's Gospel can be divided into *seven* segments, which includes a body of *five* sermons. The number *seven* comes from the

Hebrew root *savah*, which means to be full or satisfied. Within his Gospel Matthew frequently refers to the number seven when telling stories about the fullness of Jesus as Lord.

The number *five* refers to a kind of favor given to the unworthy—grace. Grace is God's gift to humanity. The five sermons in the body of Matthew's Gospel are linked to the first five books of the Old Testament. These books (Genesis, Exodus, Leviticus, Numbers and Deuteronomy) are called the Torah (Hebrew) or the Pentateuch (Greek). They are the books in which we find the teachings or the Law. *Law* here is not used in a juridical sense; rather the Law comes out of the grace-filled recognition that it is God, Yahweh, who gives life. The followers of Yahweh respond to the gift of life by living the Law in order to establish peace and justice. Matthew shows that as the Law of God is presented in the first five books of the Old Testament, the new Law of God as given by Christ is presented in five sermons.

Discovering

We can see a connection between the heart of the Old Testament and the heart of the New Testament. In the Old Testament the main story is the Exodus/Sinai event (see Exodus 1—20), the time of great liberation and covenant with God. The beginning of salvation history (Genesis 12—50), with its stories of Abraham, Isaac, Jacob and Joseph (the Patriarchs), serves as a prologue to this liberation event. All events that follow the Exodus, everything related in the historical, prophetic and wisdom writings, refer to this liberation.

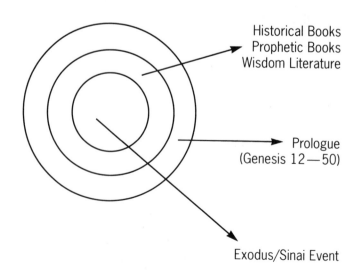

Historical Books
Prophetic Books
Wisdom Literature

Prologue
(Genesis 12—50)

Exodus/Sinai Event

The heart of the New Testament is the passion, death and resurrection of Jesus. This too is a time of great liberation and a new covenant between God and God's people. It is the primary message of the New Testament. This event fulfills the Old Testament prophecies and establishes Jesus as the Christ. The stories of Jesus' birth and the stories of his ministry are all related to this central event. Remember that Gospel writing is faith sharing and not biographical.

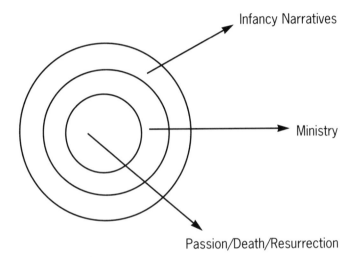

Infancy Narratives

Ministry

Passion/Death/Resurrection

Throughout his Gospel, Matthew refers to the close association between Old Testament stories and New Testament events.

Looking Back

On Journey 2 you made the following discoveries:

- Stories are important in conveying the gospel message.
- The richness of the Old Testament message is essential for understanding Matthew's Gospel.
- Numerology plays an important part in Matthew's Gospel.
- The heart of the Old Testament connects to the heart of the New Testament.

Exploring Further

Boadt, Lawrence. *Reading the Old Testament: An Introduction*. Mahwah, N.J.: Paulist Press, 1984.

Bullinger, E. W. *Number in Scripture*. Grand Rapids, Mich.: Kregel Publications, 1967.

Journey 3

Scripture as a Means of Reflection

Scripture study is a matter of the heart as well as of the head. Realizing that God's message is a message of salvation calls for transformation in one's life. When we discover biblical passages that speak to our lives, we make a religious affirmation of the principles we find there. Through action we live the truth of the message. In reflecting on the Old Testament we seek God's intimate involvement within our lives; in the New Testament we explore what it means to "put on Christ."

Discovering

Reflection exercises are strategically placed throughout the manual. They will help you come to know God and yourself more deeply. Through a series of reflections you will have the opportunity to discover the true meaning of the Journey and to speak to God with trust and openness. Do not hesitate to express to God your doubts and fears as well as your joys.

Journey 2 introduced various tools for studying Scripture. You discovered the need to understand the Old Testament as a foundation for understanding the New Testament. The following reflective exercise again brings you to the heart of the Old Testament. This exercise will lead you to the God of your own heart.

Read through the entire exercise first; then return to step 1 and follow each step to its conclusion.

1) Find a place where you can be alone to read and reflect quietly for about 45 minutes.

2) Sit in a chair with your feet flat on the floor, hands on your lap, or lie down on a rug or on the ground. Have your Bible, paper and pencil near you. You will be reading various Old Testament passages; it is helpful to mark the pages with a bookmark for easy reference.

3) Reduce the tension throughout your body by concentrating on each of your body parts in turn, starting with the soles of your feet and moving upward— feet, legs, torso, arms, shoulders, neck—until you reach the top of your head.

4) Slowly read Psalm 104.

5) Imagine yourself as the center of the universe with all creation around you. Try to incorporate within your imagination as many of your senses as possible: see the trees, feel the wind blowing, smell the flowers.

6) Read Exodus 15:1-18.

7) Reflect on the times in your life when you have felt trapped. These may be events or situations you believed were sinful, or you may have felt trapped by another's behavior or by a situation beyond your control.

8) Imagine that the event or situation that was entrapping you is plunged into the depths of a sea. It drowns and you are free.

9) Reflect on what the feeling of freedom and peace means to you.

10) Imagine God welcoming you into divine peace and freedom.

11) In any manner of prayer comfortable for you, claim God's peace as your own.

12) Reread Exodus 15:1-18.

13) Gather your pencil and paper and begin writing what you experienced during the reflection. When you have finished expressing all of your thoughts, wait a few more minutes to see if additional reflections come to consciousness.

Looking Back

In Journey 3, you made the following discoveries:

- The study of Scripture is a matter of the heart and the head.
- Reflective exercises can help you truly know the Scriptures.
- Various techniques for reflective exercises may be used as tools for imagining scriptural accounts.

Journey 4

Birth Stories

The birth of any child is a sign of hope for all humanity. It assures the continuation of the species and establishes a new generation to build the world. This joyous occasion is celebrated in thanksgiving and praise of life itself. The births of great leaders are remembered and celebrated by their followers as the beginning that makes possible the contributions such leaders make to others and to the world.

Discovering

In Scripture every account of a great king or prophet begins with the story of an extraordinary birth, which reveals the way God selected that person from the beginning.

Read the following birth stories from Scripture:
    Genesis 21:1-8;
    Exodus 2:1-10;
    Judges 13.

Exploring

The story in Genesis 21:1-8 demonstrates God's greatness in granting the aged Sarah and Abraham a son. Not only was Sarah old, she had been barren—a sign to the Jews that someone has not been blessed by God.

Similarly, in Judges 13 Manoah's wife is barren, but the angel reveals that she will bear a son, Samson. Both stories unfold God's ability to do all things, represented by the ability to make even the barren fertile. The stories of Rebekah and Rachel also tell of barren women having children (Genesis 25:21; Genesis 30:1-24).

Although Moses' mother is not barren (Exodus 2), her child is delivered at the time when Pharaoh has ordered, "Throw into the river every boy that is born to the Hebrews..." (Exodus 1:22). Moses is miraculously saved from Pharaoh's command so that later in life he can lead the Israelites out of slavery.

These three extraordinary births give us Isaac, for whom "...all the nations of the earth shall find blessing" (Genesis 22:17-18); Moses, the greatest figure of the Old Testament; and Samson, who as an adult demonstrates phenomenal strength against the Philistines.

Discovering

Matthew begins his Gospel by relating the greatest birth story of all—the birth of Christ. This great birth gives the world *Emmanuel*, Matthew's favorite name for Jesus. Read the following passages and summarize the key ideas:

Matthew 1:23

Matthew 28:20

Exploring

Matthew frames his entire Gospel with these two citations. Both relate to Jesus as Emmanuel. Matthew 1:23 presents Christ's name, *Emmanuel*, which means "God is with us." The last words of Matthew 28 conclude the Gospel with the assurance that Jesus is with us always.

Discovering

Journey 2 mentioned that Matthew's genealogy is artificially constructed as a mnemonic device relating to the three letters of the name *David*. The genealogy may be slightly different than the familiar family trees tied together by blood relatives. Scripture scholar Eugene LaVerdiere teaches that the New Testament genealogy presents all individuals—living and dead, related by blood and not—as essential characters for an individual's formation.

Matthew's genealogy presents the messianic hope that was passed down through the lineage of David and made present in Jesus who is called the Messiah. In his genealogy, Matthew lists biblical characters who announce in some way the coming of the Messiah.

Scholars often point out that four women are mentioned in Matthew's genealogy: Tamar, Rahab, Ruth and the wife of Uriah (Bathsheba). Three positions are set forth as to why these women are placed within Matthew's genealogy.

1) The four women are (or are considered to be) sinners; by inserting them in his genealogy Matthew reveals that Jesus has come for sinners and those outside the Law.

2) The women are not Jews; Matthew thus demonstrates that Jesus has come for the Gentiles.

3) The women entered into unusual unions that resulted in extraordinary events in the history of the chosen people. Their unions are compared to Mary's union with Joseph and the workings of the Holy Spirit. The stories of these women demonstrate how God intervenes in human history and upholds the promise of a Messiah despite human actions.

Discovering

Matthew's birth story provides an overture to his whole Gospel. Joseph and the Magi play key roles in this story.

The following verses are keys to Joseph's significance:

Matthew 1:19-21, 24-25;
Matthew 2:13-14, 19-23.

Exploring

Matthew believed that those listening to the biblical story would see the connection between Joseph of the New Testament and Joseph of the Old Testament (Genesis 30—50).

In the Old Testament Joseph receives messages in dreams (Genesis 37:5-11) and also interprets dreams (Genesis 40—41). He is the last Patriarch who brings the Israelites to Egypt. As Joseph's story ends, the reader is introduced to the Exodus event and Moses, the most famous Old Testament figure. Moses is hidden after his birth because of Pharaoh's threat. In his adult years Moses leads the Israelites from slavery to the new land flowing with milk and honey.

In the New Testament Joseph receives messages in dreams (Matthew 1:24; 2:13; 2:19; and 2:22). He is an upright man who accepts Jesus as his son, indicated by his naming of Jesus (Matthew 1:25). Like Joseph of the Old Testament, he brings Jesus, the new Israel, to Egypt because of Herod's threat. As Jesus begins his ministry as an adult we discover that he is greater than Moses, that he will lead all people out of the slavery of sin and death.

Discovering

Read Matthew 2:1-12.

Exploring

Matthew's introduction of the astrologers may be his attempt to highlight the Gentiles of his community. The astrologers come from a non-Jewish place; they interpret the Hebrew Scriptures of Isaiah 60:6 and Psalm 72:10-11; they worship the Christ. The Gentiles of Matthew's community, like the Magi, are aware of the Hebrew Scriptures and the passages that foretell the Messiah. They accept Jesus as the Christ.

The star that leads the astrologers echoes the Old Testament story of Balaam: "A star shall advance from Jacob, and a staff shall rise from Israel..." (Numbers 24:17). The star also suggests the belief that at the birth of every great leader a new star is born in the heavens.

The astrologers, who are men of wisdom, come and bow down before the Child-king. They offer gifts, as is customary at the birth of a great leader. The gifts—gold, frankincense and myrrh—relate to Isaiah 60:6: "Caravans of camels shall fill you,/dromedaries from Midian and Ephah;/All from Sheba shall come/bearing gold and frankincense,/and proclaiming the praises of the LORD."

Looking Back

On Journey 4 you made the following discoveries:

- Birth stories are important in recounting the lives of great leaders.
- The genealogy of Matthew presents significant people who foretell the coming of the Messiah.
- Connections exist between Joseph of the New Testament and Joseph of the Old Testament.
- The Magi are Gentile (non-Jewish) people of wisdom who recognize that Jesus is the Christ.

Exploring Further

Brown, Raymond E. *The Birth of the Messiah*, rev. ed. New York: Doubleday, 1993.

Journey 5

Jesus Begins His Ministry

The *New American Bible* introduces Matthew 3 with the subtitle: *The Proclamation of the Kingdom.* Matthew divides the main portion of his Gospel into five sermons, each beginning with a preparatory narrative. Chapters 3 and 4 contain the narrative that leads to the Kingdom sermon found in Matthew 5.

Discovering

John announces the coming of the Kingdom.

Read and summarize the major points of Malachi 3:22-24.

Read and summarize the major points of 2 Kings 1:8 and Matthew 3:4.

Exploring

The reading from Malachi says that Elijah will be sent to change peoples' hearts before the Lord will come. 2 Kings 1:8 and Matthew 3:4 show similarity in the clothing of Elijah and John the Baptist. These references point to John as the Elijah figure who prepares the way of the Lord.

Discovering

Read Matthew 17:10-13.

Exploring

Following the Transfiguration, Jesus is quick to point out that the Elijah figure has indeed come in the person of John the Baptist. So clear is Jesus in this regard that even the disciples understand that Jesus is speaking of John.

Discovering

Read Matthew 3:1-12.

Write one word that captures the essence of John's preaching.

Exploring

John emphasizes the need for repentance: "Repent, for the kingdom of heaven is at hand" (Matthew 3:2). Repentance suggests a need for reform, a movement or transition from one form of life to another. The person who is *reformed* abandons harmful ways of behavior in order to embrace that which is good. John instructs his listeners that with the Kingdom of God at hand (that which is good), they must abandon past behavior (that which is harmful or sinful). This instruction will be clarified in the Beatitudes (Matthew 5).

Discovering

The account of Jesus' Baptism provides an opportunity to introduce a popular theory regarding the formation of Gospel materials. Matthew, Mark and Luke are referred to as Synoptic Gospels. Recall that the term *synoptic* comes from two Greek words (*syn*=one, *optic*=look) and means "a seeing together." These three Gospels report similar events in Jesus' life, death and resurrection. We can put the Gospels in three side-by-side columns and get three variations of many of the same accounts.

Read Matthew 3:13-17.
Read Mark 1:9-11.
Read Luke 3:21-22.

Exploring

Notice the similarity in these three accounts of the Baptism. Biblical scholars noticed other similarities among Matthew, Mark and Luke. Some scholars claim that approximately 70 percent of Matthew's material is similar to the material found in Mark's Gospel. The most widely accepted theory claims that Mark was the first writer (around 70 C.E.) and Matthew and Luke (around 85 C.E.) borrowed from him.

Biblical scholars also noticed that some material is common to both Matthew and Luke ("M" and "L" below) but does not appear in Mark.

Read Matthew 3:7-10 and Luke 3:7-9.

From this example and others, it appears Matthew and Luke shared another source containing Jesus' sayings. Scripture scholars refer to this source as the "Q" source, from the German word *quelle*, which means source.

A further comparison of the synoptic material reveals that some stories are found only in Matthew and not the other writers. For example, only Matthew's Gospel includes the following stories: the weeds (Matthew 13:24-30); the treasure and the pearl (13:44-46); the net (13:47-50); the merciless official (18:23-25); the laborers in the vineyard (20:1-16); the two sons (21:28-32); the wedding banquet (22:1-14); the ten virgins (25:1-13); the last judgment (25:31-46).

This kind of comparison led to the theory that Matthew gathered his material from Mark, "Q" and his own sources. The diagram below illustrates this theory:

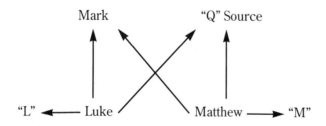

Discovering

Read Matthew 4:1-11, Mark 1:12-13 and Luke 4:1-13.

In the space provided write the similarities and differences you discover in the three accounts of the temptation of Jesus.

Similarities

Differences

Exploring

One similarity you may notice is that the Spirit drove Jesus into the desert where he was tempted by the devil for forty days. The reference to *desert* and *forty* corresponds to the Israelites wandering in the desert for forty years after escaping from Pharaoh and his armies.

Matthew and Luke elaborate on the devil's temptations, whereas Mark simply says Jesus was tempted. We may conclude that the elaboration found in Matthew and Luke is "Q" material.

Discovering

In the space provided write what you believe is the essence of Satan's temptations.

1)

2)

3)

Exploring

Compare your work with mine.

1) Son of God — stones into bread;

2) Son of God — throw self down from the Temple;

3) Son of God — given the world as a reward for worshipping evil.

The first two temptations specifically refer to Jesus as Son of God. (We may assume the title is implied in the third temptation.) While the title "Son of God" has many meanings it does not mean biological son of the Father. A biological relationship would erroneously imply that the Father existed before the Son, which is contrary to our belief in the Trinity.

The title Son of God used together with the desert setting and the forty days' timespan may suggest a connection to the Exodus event and a comparison between Jesus and the Israelites. Jesus is the new Israel; unlike the Israelites in the desert, who abandoned God by worshiping a golden calf (see Exodus 32), Jesus rebukes Satan with principles from Deuteronomy 6—8.

Read Deuteronomy 6—8.

Deuteronomy 6:4-5 is known as the Shema (from the Hebrew word *shema*, meaning "to hear") and is regarded as the core of the Law. Jesus refers to loving God with one's whole heart, soul and might, that is, one's whole being. Scholars say *heart* refers to one's choice between good and evil; *soul* refers to one's willingness to give up one's life; *might* refers to the sacrifice of all of one's possessions. Therefore, right choices, all of life and all one's possessions equal a total giving of oneself to God.

Matthew's Gospel shows how the life of Jesus demonstrates the way to obey the Deuteronomic Law. Those who hear the gospel message must worship God with their whole being. Turning stones to bread and leaping from high buildings are spectacular feats unable to be accomplished by humans; they are god-acts. Jesus resists the temptation to put on a display and remains faithful in his loyalty to the Father.

Matthew may be reminding his community (and all believers) that many will be tempted away from God. True believers, like Jesus, will always remain faithful in their loyalty to the Father.

Looking Back

On Journey 5 you made the following discoveries:

- Matthew uses the following sources to write his Gospel: Mark, "Q" and a unique source.
- The Baptism of Jesus introduces John as the Elijah figure.
- The temptations of Jesus are rooted in the Old Testament Exodus event.
- The responses from Deuteronomy 6—8 that Jesus uses to combat Satan are the same responses that all Christians must make.

Exploring Further

The New Jerome Biblical Commentary, rev. ed. Raymond E. Brown, Joseph Fitzmyer, Roland Murphy, eds. Englewood Cliffs, N.J.: Prentice Hall, 1990.

Journey 6

The Sermon on the Mount: The Kingdom

In the space provided, write your understanding of the Kingdom of God. If you want an additional challenge, write your understanding of the Kingdom of God for a stranger who is a nonbeliever.

Exploring

For many "Kingdom of God" refers to heaven; it is not seen as the heart and center of Jesus' preaching. Yet Matthew presents Jesus primarily as the one who announces the Kingdom of God.

Discovering

Read Matthew 5:1-12.
Read Matthew 11:11-13.
Read Matthew 24:14.

Exploring

Theologian Richard McBrien defines the Kingdom of God as "the redemptive presence of God" or "the saving presence of God" ("What Is 'The Kingdom of God'?" *Catholic Update*). According to McBrien, whenever people demonstrate their love, forgiveness and compassion for others, the redemptive presence of God is manifested.

The Kingdom of God began with creation when the presence of God was manifested in creation itself.

Obviously the Kingdom of God came into creation most decisively with Jesus the Christ. The living God is actively involved in people's lives; the Kingdom of God is now. The Kingdom is striving for perfection; it will be manifested in this perfection when Christ comes again. As believers and followers of Matthew's message, we are to proclaim that the Kingdom of God has begun, is now present and continues to unfold.

Discovering

Reread Matthew 5:1-2.

In the space provided, write the setting and action.

Exploring

The setting—Jesus on the mountainside—is reminiscent of Moses and the covenant given on Mt. Sinai (Exodus 19:20). The Law God gave to Moses is being replaced by the new law Christ gives to his disciples. Jesus sits before his disciples, the traditional posture of a teacher in his day; this is a sign of his authority.

Discovering

In the space provided write one or two sentences that capture the essence of each Beatitude. A hint: Consider how each Beatitude depends on the preceding one(s).

1) poor in spirit

7) peacemakers

2) those who mourn

8) persecuted

3) meek

Exploring

In the *New American Bible* each Beatitude begins with the word *blessed*; other translations use *happy* or *fortunate*. A beatitude is a blessing God bestows on a person for a position taken in life. In a sense God's blessing is a cosmic force that takes on its own reality. Think of the first creation story in Genesis: God says, "Let there be light," and light appears. Old Testament references to beatitudes may be found in Proverbs 3:13 and Proverbs 28:14.

4) hunger and thirst for righteousness

1) Poor in spirit. Read Deuteronomy 15:7-11 and Isaiah 61:1 for background to understanding "poor in spirit." The poor (*anawim*) are favored by God not because of their economic status, but rather because they see all gifts as coming from God. The poor in spirit are humble; they know that possessions and material goods have no power or satisfaction when compared to the gifts given by God. No matter what the financial situation, the God of one's heart is always Yahweh.

5) merciful

2) Mourning. Isaiah 61:2c-3 proclaims the prophet's mission: to "comfort all who mourn;/To place on those who mourn in Zion/a diadem [crown] instead of ashes." Isaiah's concern is for those who mourn the destruction of the Temple by the Babylonians, which began the great diaspora. Likewise, Matthew's Beatitude comforts those who mourn the times they did not hold God as the center of their heart, but placed other gods in their hearts. (Remember heart refers to the choices of life, especially the choice between good and evil.) Choices we made in the past can never be relived. We also mourn for the world's sinfulness.

6) clean of heart

3) Meek. The term *meek* has its Old Testament background in Psalm 37: "But the poor will possess the land,/will delight in great prosperity" (Psalm 37:11). Like the "poor in spirit" (first Beatitude), the "meek" are humble and realize their true relationship with God.

God is the creator of all; no one aspect of creation is better than another. All creation recognizes God as Father. The question that captures the humbling quality of this Beatitude is, "Of all the possibilities God could have created, why did God create me?"

4) Hunger and thirst for righteousness. The Old Testament backdrop for this passage may be found in Psalm 107:5-9. Matthew also encourages covenant fidelity. We are called to create a world that reflects the intentions and desires of God. God intends all men and women to be brothers and sisters, equally deserving of respect and dignity. We are to hunger and thirst, that is, to desire to create a godly environment. The Beatitude rightly suggests that we are never filled with God, but constantly seek to receive more of God.

5) Merciful. Proverb 14:21 says the one who is kind to the poor is happy. This kindness is not pity but mercy, the attribute of God. Read the stories of Genesis 3—11. In each of the four accounts a person chooses sin, which leads to a form of death. Each story, however, ends not with death, but rather with an action that demonstrates God's mercy: Eve is made the mother of humankind; Cain given a protective mark; Noah's family survives the flood; Abraham is called into a covenant with God. Mercy is the realization that *all* people are brothers and sisters to us—*even* the poor, the disabled, the outcasts and prostitutes. The Jesus of Matthew's Gospel constantly lives this Beatitude.

Discovering

In the space provided, write how Jesus demonstrates this Beatitude in each of the following accounts.

Matthew 5:43-47

Matthew 9:13

Matthew 12:7

Matthew 18:35

Matthew 23:23

Matthew 25:31-46

Exploring

6) Clean of heart. Psalm 24:3 asks, "Who may go up the mountain of the LORD?/ Who can stand in his holy place?" The next verse responds: "The clean of hand and pure of heart...." Psalm 24 is the foundation for this Beatitude. Those who are pure of heart move toward the truth—a truth only found in God. In moving toward truth, one moves with integrity toward covenant justice and love. The perfect example is Jesus, who is so one with the Father that no person, being or object will deter him from the path of truth set forth by the Father.

7) Peacemakers. When the late Mary Reed Newland, noted catechist and storyteller, spoke of peace and justice, she always defined the terms as "the way God is." The peace and justice of God is achieved when the most alienated of people come together as brother and sister and live together in a harmony that reflects "the way God is." The Beatitude encourages everyone to be like Christ, actively pursuing peace on earth as the means of building the Kingdom.

8) Persecuted. When we make a choice for what is good, we also reject something evil or wrong. Likewise, when we follow Christ on the journey to the Father, we reject Satan and all that is evil. When we bring together in love those who previously hated each other, we demonstrate the truth; we reject the lie of hatred and malice. Evil, however, does not give up easily. It will do everything in its power to ostracize, condemn and cause pain to those who are peacemakers. Our good name, our person and/or our families will be attacked.

Matthew may be speaking to his community here. They were being ostracized and attacked because of their belief in Jesus as Lord. But he is also speaking to all communities. We can expect to be rejected by society if we attempt to make God's teachings a reality.

Looking Back

On Journey 6 you made the following discoveries:

- Jesus' first sermon is on the Kingdom of God.
- The Kingdom of God is God's redemptive presence.
- The Kingdom of God is presented in the Sermon on the Mount.
- Each of the Beatitudes is rooted in Old Testament passages.
- The Christian who lives the Beatitudes can expect to be persecuted and hated by those who follow evil.

Exploring Further

McBrien, Richard. "What Is 'The Kingdom of God'?" *Catholic Update*. Cincinnati, Ohio: St. Anthony Messenger Press, September 1980.

Lachs, Samuel Tobias. *A Rabbinic Commentary on the New Testament: The Gospels of Matthew, Mark and Luke*. Hoboken, N.J.: Ktav Publishing House, Inc., 1987.

Journey 7

The Kingdom Sermon Continues

The core of Matthew's sermon on the Kingdom is presented in 5:1-12. Here the Christian believer discovers what is essential for following Christ. The phrase "Christian Manifesto," coined by Scripture scholar Neil Flanagan, captures the essence of this passage. Matthew, in presenting the Beatitudes as the Christian Manifesto, lays the foundation for Christians to publicly proclaim their intention to follow Jesus and build the Kingdom of God. The "sayings" that follow Matthew 5:1-12 exemplify and elaborate on the Beatitudes.

Discovering

Read Matthew 5:13-16.

Exploring

Matthew 5:13-16 describes disciples as "salt of the earth" and "light of the world." In Matthew 10 an entire sermon is dedicated to discipleship.

In biblical times salt was used to preserve and season food. Salt cannot lose its flavor, but within Jewish Law salt could become unclean and thus would have to be discarded. The disciple, as a teacher, must never lose his or her real purpose by becoming unclean. Rather, the disciple must continue to "preserve" the word of God by passing it on to students. This action will properly "season" the students' minds and hearts.

Homes were large, one-room dwellings shared by extended families and sometimes even strangers. Both those wealthy enough to provide fuel for lamps and those inhabitants who could not afford fuel literally lived in the light cast from the one household lamp placed on a high stand. The disciple, like the lamp, is to give light for all.

Discovering

Read Matthew 5:17-20.

Exploring

Jesus clearly states that he has not come to abolish the Old Testament Law. Matthew's community was rooted in Jewish tradition. As the Christian message spread, two things influenced the community: (1) an influx of Gentiles who did not know Jewish Law, and (2) hostility from other Jews who did not recognize Jesus as the Messiah. In the midst of change and turmoil Matthew may be telling his community that Jesus is the fulfillment of the Law and thus accomplishes the goal set forth by God. Matthew asks the question, "Where do we find the teaching, law and love of God?" He answers the question by constantly pointing to Jesus. Matthew reveals that everything God has planned for us is found in Jesus the Christ.

Discovering

Read Matthew 5:21-48.

The section highlights a popular literary form called "antithesis," in which the writer first presents one statement and immediately follows it with an opposing point of view, for example, "You have heard...but I say." We can find another example in 1 Corinthians 15:22, where Paul contrasts death in Adam with life in Christ.

In the space below write the antitheses presented in Matthew 5:21-48. Place the commandment and/or practice from the Old Testament against the new challenge presented by Jesus.

Commandment/Practice

Jesus' Challenge

Exploring

Compare your contrasts with mine.

Commandment/Practice

1) no murder
2) no adultery
3) divorce permitted for men
4) take solemn oath
5) legal parity
6) hate your enemies
7) public piety merely for show
8) trust in earthly possessions
9) hypocritical judging

Jesus' Challenge

1) no anger
2) no lust
3) respect for wife
4) no swearing at all
5) no retaliation
6) love your enemies
7) rivate prayer, almsgiving and fasting
8) trust in God
9) personal repentance and conversion

Matthew 5:21-48 provides a commentary on the antitheses that bring the believer beyond the surface of the statement to the heart of God's message. In the antitheses the disciple will discover the true message of God: love, mercy and truth.

In the verses prior to the section, Matthew states that one's holiness must surpass the Pharisees and scribes (Matthew 5:20). The difficulty is not that one is a Pharisee or a scribe; rather it was wrong to assume an attitude that places more emphasis on the Law than on God. The Law, which was to be a loving response to God's revelation, had at times become an end in itself, especially among some of the Pharisees. When we place ourselves above the Law we can easily become hypocrites. This condition is diametrically opposed to being "poor in spirit" or "meek," where we realize the true law is God and all people are our brothers and sisters.

Matthew places on the lips of Jesus the words "You have heard that it was said...but I say" to remind listeners that Jesus, like the Father, is the one who truly gives the Law.

1) Although the Law says no murder (Matthew 5:21), Jesus carries this further by challenging listeners to eliminate or control the root of murder, which is anger. Again, the challenge goes beyond external practice of the Law to include inner attitudes and intentions.

2, 3) The true intention of the Law is also witnessed in the challenge concerning adultery and divorce (Matthew 5:27). Just as murder may begin with anger, adultery begins with lust. The person whose heart is filled with lust has lost respect for the dignity of the other person. The ideal relationship between man and woman is presented in the Genesis account: "God created man in his image; in the divine image he created him; male and female he created them" (1:27).

The exception, "unless the marriage is unlawful" (Matthew 5:32), has baffled Scripture scholars for some time. Scholars note that Matthew's Greek term is *porneia* rather than *moicheuo*. The word *moicheuo* refers to "adultery," while the word *porneia* is used for "incestuous relationships," and so on. By using *porneia* in this case Matthew upholds the Law of Leviticus 18:6-18, which forbids incestuous relationships, while offering a new challenge that would not permit divorce for any other reason.

Another Old Testament reference is found in Deuteronomy 24:1-4, which permits a man to write a bill of divorce from his wife for matters of indecency. In Matthew 19:8, Jesus reminds the Pharisees that Moses permitted divorce because of the hardness of men's hearts. Furthermore, during Matthew's time, an ongoing dispute on divorce was lead by two rabbinical schools: Hillel and Shammai. The Hillel school permitted divorce for any reason, whereas the Shammai school limited divorce to cases of female impurity. Matthew may be upholding the Shammai interpretation for his community or may be clarifying the meaning of impurity.

4) The challenge not to swear or make oaths at all is radical; it appears to be directly opposed to the Law as stated in Exodus 20:7 or Leviticus 19:12. Matthew may be linking his statement in 5:34 with statements he makes in 23:16-22. The taking of an oath was to verify the truth. Yet Matthew 23:16-22 demonstrates how the Pharisees and scribes have twisted the taking of oaths to justify avoiding the truth. Rather than eliminating the Law, Jesus emphasizes its true meaning.

Matthew also reminds his readers that God is the "ultimate other" and is beyond the comprehension of mere humans. Humans have no right to call on God to witness anything. Humans can only love and obey the Lord.

5) Three Old Testament references (Exodus 21:22-25, Leviticus 24:20, Deuteronomy 19:21) lay the ground rule against revenge and retaliation, the point of the next antithesis. The statement "an eye for an eye, and a tooth for a tooth" is often misinterpreted today in order to permit retaliation. The Old Testament Law required a just means of reciprocity and was written in order to keep people's actions in balance. Jesus goes beyond even this balanced treatment and commands his followers to love even their enemies.

6) Both the Old Testament (Psalm 139:19-22) and Qumran material upheld that hatred of evil persons was assumed to be right. Jesus extended the love commandment to the enemy and the persecutor. Jesus' disciples, as children of God, must imitate the example of their Father, who grants gifts to the good and bad alike. Again, Jesus challenges his hearers to live a radical lifestyle that provides a glimpse of what the Kingdom of God is like.

7, 8, 9) All of the antitheses presented by Jesus are ways to establish the Kingdom of God, which will transform the world. Each of the challenges is Jesus' way of pointing to the endtime when the Kingdom will be fulfilled.

The sermon concludes with an entire section on purity of intentions (Matthew 6) which is parallel to the Holiness Code of Leviticus (17—26). The ultimate witness for living a holy life is prayer, almsgiving and fasting. Prayer establishes a true relationship between humans and God. Almsgiving is a concrete way to live the belief that all women and men are sisters and brothers. Fasting has its Old Testament roots in Isaiah 58:6-7, which states: "This, rather, is the fasting that I wish:/ releasing those bound unjustly, untying the thongs of the yoke;/ Setting free the oppressed, breaking every yoke;/ Sharing your bread with the hungry,/ sheltering the oppressed and the homeless;/ Clothing the naked when you see them,/ and not turning your back on your own." When one fasts with these intentions in mind, one humbles oneself before God and is ready to serve others.

Looking Back

On Journey 7 you made the following discoveries:

- The sermon on the Kingdom provides guidelines for how a disciple should live.
- Matthew provides an antithesis to the Old

Testament Law in order to demonstrate the true meaning of the Law.
- The follower of Jesus adopts the radical life-style presented by Jesus.
- The ultimate witness to a holy life is prayer, fasting and almsgiving.

Exploring Further

Kingsbury, Jack Dean, ed. *The Gospel of Matthew. Interpretation: A Journal of Bible and Theology*, vol. XLVI, October 1992.

Meier, John P. *Matthew,* New Testament Message, vol. 3. Collegeville, Minn.: Michael Glazier, 1980.

Journey 8

Reflections on Your Journey

Journeys 6 and 7 presented the foundation of Jesus' preaching on the Kingdom of God. Like Jesus' disciples, we are called to bring about the Kingdom of God. Certainly the challenges for establishing the Kingdom of God that Matthew's first sermon presents are different from the challenges offered by modern society. The radical life-style Matthew presents for his community must be lived out in our day. Journey 8 is a reflective exercise that asks us to accept Jesus' radical challenges.

Read through the entire exercise in order to become comfortable with the steps. Then do the exercise.

Discovering

1) Find a place that is relatively quiet. You will need at least 40 minutes to perform this exercise.

2) Sit in a chair with your feet flat on the floor, your hands in your lap, your back straight, your eyes lowered or closed. Keep a pencil and paper nearby.

3) Relax your body by concentrating on your breathing. Begin by imagining that you are inhaling light, peace and relaxation and exhaling fear, anxiety and darkness. Attempt to establish a slow, steady rhythm of inhaling and exhaling.

4) In your mind's eye, go to a place—real or imaginary—where you can relax. It may be in the mountains or at the seashore or another place in which you find calmness and peace. In your imagination invite Jesus to this place. Discuss with Jesus what you believe to be the difference between the values of society and the values of the Kingdom. Ask Jesus for ways in which you might change some values in your life-style that are contrary to Kingdom values.

5) When you finish this imaginary conversation list the values of society and the values of the Kingdom. Next to any society value you believe you need to change in your life, jot down a few ideas that will help you make the transition from one value to the other.

Exploring

Here are some of the contrasting values that I have used for personal reflection. I offer them merely as aids for doing the reflection. Remember, there are no right or wrong answers on this Journey.

Society's Values

1) faith as an outward expression of worship
2) lead or make your own way
3) when the cat's away, the mice will play
4) be boisterous
5) put on a good show
6) it's OK as long as you don't hurt anyone
7) hate those who hurt you
8) cynicism
9) greed
10) look for future rewards
11) judge others

Kingdom Values

1) inner personal faith
2) be a servant
3) prepare for the Lord
4) be introspective
5) don't be a hypocrite
6) correct one another
7) forgive
8) trust
9) gratitude
10) live each moment fully
11) personal repentance

Looking Back

On Journey 8 you made the following discoveries:

- Society teaches values that are different than Kingdom values.
- Reflecting on these differences can show us where we need to make changes in our life-style.

Journey 9

Discipleship

We have seen that the body of Matthew's Gospel can be divided into five sermons. The first sermon (presented in Journeys 5-7) lays the foundation for the Christian message, which is the Kingdom of God. For the Kingdom to spread, workers (disciples) need to present the message to others.

The first followers of Jesus are referred to as apostles (Matthew 10:2). The term *apostle* has its roots in a semitic word that originally meant "one commissioned by the king to fulfill a mission in his name and in his authority." After Jesus' resurrection the early Church uses the term *apostle* for the original twelve who were intimate followers of Jesus and who were eyewitnesses to his works.

The emphasis on *twelve* is deliberate. It not only represents the literal number of Jesus' closest associates, it also has symbolic significance, suggesting the twelve tribes of Israel and the twelve judgment seats described in Matthew 19:28. These two references, as well as other biblical citations, suggest that the number twelve represents perfect government or perfect rule.

Discovering

Scripture refers to the disciples or followers of Jesus. At that time some individuals left home and family to answer a call to follow someone they believed preached the truth. In both the Old and New Testaments we can discover and list six characteristics of such calls.

1) A call is pure gift; the individual does nothing to deserve the call.

2) A call is unique and directed to an individual.

3) A call enables a person to develop his or her full potential.

4) A call is a process that moves an individual into ever deeper stages of following.

5) A call moves a person from the known to the unknown.

6) A call is for others within the community, never merely for the individual.

Reread Matthew 4:18-22.

In the space provided, write the characteristics of a call that can be identified within this passage.

Exploring

The call of Peter and Andrew is pure gift. They are merely casting nets, doing nothing out of the ordinary to merit a call.

The call was unique and directed to individuals. Jesus calls Peter, Andrew, James and John.

The call enables these Galilean fishermen to develop potentials of which they may have been unaware.

Within the scene the men move from the known to the unknown as they abandon their boats and their father to follow Jesus to a place they do not know.

The call is for others in the community. Jesus tells them that he will "make [them] fishers of men" (verse 19). The two sets of brothers join together to become part of the community of Christ.

Discovering

The actual introduction to Matthew's sermon on discipleship begins with Matthew 8.

Read Matthew 8:1—9:34.

Briefly summarize the events presented in the following scriptural passages. Place an asterisk (*) by those events that are miracles.

8:1-4

8:28-34

8:5-13

9:1-8

8:14-15

9:9-13

8:16-17

9:14-17

8:18-22

9:18-26

8:23-27

9:27-31

9:32-34

Exploring

Did you place an asterisk by the following miracle events:

- 8:1-4: curing a leper;
- 8:5-13: curing the centurion's servant;
- 8:14-15: curing Peter's mother-in-law;
- 8:16-17: curing many who were possessed;
- 8:23-27: calming the sea;
- 8:28-34: curing two men possessed with demons;
- 9:1-8: curing a man who was paralyzed;
- 9:18-26: raising a dead girl and curing a woman with a hemorrhage;
- 9:27-31: curing two blind men;
- 9:32-34: curing a possessed mute.

Discovering

Some scholars pay special attention to the fact that ten miracle stories are presented here. They compare them to the Ten Commandments presented in Exodus 20 as another example of Jesus giving a new law. Whether this connection was deliberate on Matthew's part is still heavily debated. The majority of scholars, however, accept an Old Testament foundation for the miracle stories.

Read Isaiah 26:19; 29:18-19; 35:4-6; 53:4.

What connection, if any, can you make between the ten miracle stories of Matthew and the four passages from Isaiah? Write your answer in the space provided below.

Exploring

Isaiah 26:19 promises that the dead shall live. We see a connection with the raising of the dead girl in Matthew 9:18-26.

Isaiah 29 refers to the deaf being able to hear and the blind being able to see, a definite connection with Matthew 9:27-34.

Isaiah 35 also refers to the blind being able to see, and adds that the lame will leap and the dumb will sing. This passage connects with Matthew 9:1-8, the healing of the paralytic.

Isaiah 53:4 sums up the entire disposition of Jesus presented within the ten healing stories. Jesus shows his compassion for humankind, his willingness to bear infirmities and endure suffering, his desire that humankind be whole.

While literal healing is not to be denied, the healing stories are also more than literal. The message is that all who are spiritually blind, deaf, mute, lame and even dead are called to wholeness so that they may see Christ, hear the word, speak the message, spread the gospel and live a life in Christ.

In this prelude to the sermon on discipleship Matthew may be laying a foundation for the life of a disciple, that is, the disciple's life is to be made whole in order that the disciple might bring the message of Christ so that others may also be whole.

The wholeness of discipleship is connected to Matthew 5:48, which says, "So be perfect, just as your heavenly Father is perfect." This perfection is not merely the absence of sin. The Hebrew word for perfection used here means "whole" or "integral." The terms *perfect* and *whole* used interchangeably can be found in various Old Testament accounts, for example, Psalm 19:8 (the Law) and Ezekiel 28:12 (cities). In saying "be perfect as your heavenly Father is perfect," Matthew's Jesus speaks of the Old Testament concept of wholeness. The follower of Christ must be a whole person, someone who conforms perfectly to the definition of what a true disciple represents: one who is free from the spiritual infirmities listed in the healing stories.

Discovering

The stories that do not involve miracles have an important message as well. The miracle of calming the seas (Matthew 8:23-27) is another example of connecting the action of Jesus with the action of God. In the first creation story (Genesis 1:1—2:4) God controls the seas and demonstrates power over nature. In Matthew 8:23-27 Jesus performs a similar action, which causes those of "little faith" to be dumbfounded. Some members of Matthew's community (as well as members of some communities today) may have struggled to follow Christ's example. Matthew instructs his listeners that if they wish to be disciples, they cannot be of "little faith," nor can they be "dumbfounded" by Jesus' actions.

Looking Back

On Journey 9 you made the following discoveries:

- The term *apostle* is reserved for the original twelve and was used primarily after the Resurrection.
- A scriptural call has six characteristics.
- The healing miracles demonstrate how the disciple must be spiritually whole.
- To be perfect is to be whole, as the heavenly Father is whole.

Exploring Further

Ellis, Peter F. *Matthew: His Mind and Message,* 4th printing. Collegeville, Minn.: The Liturgical Press, 1985.

Journey 10
Sermon on Discipleship

Each of Matthew's sermons begins with a narrative that leads to the sermon. Recall that in Journey 8 we explored the narrative that introduces the sermon on discipleship. Matthew 10 presents the sermon itself.

Discovering

Read Matthew 10 according to the following three divisions. In the space provided summarize in your own words the action or instruction presented in each division.

Matthew 10:1-4

Matthew 10:5-15

Matthew 10:16-25

Exploring

The action in Matthew 10:1-4 is twofold: Jesus gives authority to the apostles and the apostles are named.

We find connections to Matthew 10:1 in Matthew 9:35-38 and Matthew 4:23-25. Jesus has authority to proclaim the good news and to heal; he passes on this authority to the disciples, who are the good laborers.

Commissioning the apostles with the authority of Jesus answers the prayer of Matthew 9:37: "...ask the master of the harvest to send out laborers for his harvest."

Matthew 10:2-4 lists the names of the apostles. All Gospel writers list Peter's name first, but vary the order of the other apostles. The emphasis on "first, Simon" may introduce the major role Peter will play in Matthew 14 and 16.

Matthew the tax collector (10:3) is most likely the same one whose story is told in Matthew 9:9-13. Tax collectors collaborated with the Roman authorities against their own people. It was not uncommon for tax collectors to extort monies in order to take care of their own needs. Hated by many, tax collectors (along with those in other professions such as tanners and camel-drivers) were considered unclean according to the Jewish Law and therefore sinners.

It is interesting to note that among the apostles are Matthew the tax collector and Simon, the Zealot party member. Zealots were a political-religious group who actively fought to overthrow the Roman government. The revolutionaries of the day, Zealots more than most would have despised tax collectors. This pairing is another example of how the Kingdom of God challenges all to live in peace and justice.

Exploring

Matthew 10:5-15 contains two major points: (1) the limitation of the mission and (2) instructions for undertaking the mission. The limitation of the mission is presented in 10:6: "Go rather to the lost sheep of the house of Israel" and is repeated in the story of Jesus' conversation with the Canaanite woman (Matthew 15:24). Both Matthew 10:6 and 15:24 attest to Jesus' earthly mission to the lost sheep of the house of Israel. No account has Jesus evangelizing out of his own area. The mission will be expanded, however, by the resurrected Christ, who sends disciples to all nations (Matthew 28:16-20).

The first instruction is to proclaim: "The kingdom of heaven is at hand." This proclamation is similar to John the Baptist's proclamation in Matthew 3:2 and Jesus' proclamation in Matthew 4:17. The linkage is deliberate on Matthew's part, showing that the disciple has the authority to carry on the work of Jesus, which was foretold by John.

The second instruction is to make the people *whole*, a

point discussed in Journey 8.

The third instruction presents a manner of dress and behavior. Ancient rabbinical works (for example, *Mishna Bekorot*) instruct the individual as to the proper attire for entering the temple. One does not wear traveling apparel or carry gold. Jesus' ban on certain clothing and possessions for his disciples is similar to such rabbinical admonitions.

The core of the missionary instruction is on *worthy* behavior: "The laborer deserves his keep." One enters the home of a *worthy* individual, that is, one who accepts both the messenger and the message.

Exploring

Matthew 10:16-25 appears to switch from the actions of the historical Jesus in the limited region of Galilee to the missionary activity of a more universal community ("...you will be led before governors and kings..."). In accepting Jesus' authority to preach, the disciple also accepts persecution and death. This message mirrors the Beatitude, "Blessed are you when they insult you and persecute you..." (Matthew 5:11).

The community of Matthew, like the rest of the early Church, lived in a time of great persecution. Within a short period of time, the Jewish-Roman wars (66-70 C.E.) resulted in the razing of Jerusalem and the Temple, the expulsion of the Christian Jews from the synagogues and the Roman persecution of the followers of Christ. In such a time of possible despair Matthew offers hope to all who acknowledge Christ.

Exploring

The final section of the sermon (Matthew 10:40-42) speaks of the need for a proper attitude. The true disciple has a welcoming attitude and is willing to welcome the "little ones." The welcoming referred to here is the same as that in Matthew 10:10-11; 31.

A word must be said regarding the difficult passage found in Matthew 10:34: "Do not think that I have come to bring peace...." Certainly, the passage cannot contradict all that Matthew has been saying regarding the love of enemies and being a peacemaker. Rather it refers to the need to decide ultimately whether or not to follow Christ. The true believer cannot be a fence sitter (like some of the Pharisees and scribes) but must proclaim absolutely that Jesus is Lord and follow the example established by Jesus.

To conclude the Journey on discipleship, reflect on the plan of action you will take to demonstrate your own willingness to proclaim the Kingdom of God. After a time of silent prayer, write those ideas that come to consciousness.

Looking Back

In Journey 10 you made the following discoveries:

- The apostles receive their authority from Jesus.
- Those called to be disciples, regardless of their background, must work to build the Kingdom of God.
- Disciples announce that the Kingdom is near and serve out of their wholeness.
- Disciples have a welcoming attitude toward all people in the Kingdom of God.
- Disciples are called to make the ultimate choice of following or not following Christ.

Exploring Further

Harrington, Daniel J. *The Gospel of Matthew,* Sacra Pagina series, vol. 1. Collegeville, Minn.: The Liturgical Press, 1991.

Kingsbury, Jack Dean. *Matthew,* Proclamation Commentaries. Philadelphia: Fortress Press, 1977.

Journey 11

Sermon on the Mystery of the Reign of God (Parables)

Matthew's first sermon lays the foundation of the Christian message; workers (disciples) are gathered and formed in the second sermon. The time has come to spread the message and Matthew prepares a sermon on the best technique for delivering the word of God—parables. Parables were a popular teaching tool during the time of Jesus; biblical scholars find approximately forty examples of parables within the Gospels.

Discovering

The word *parable* can be traced to the Greek word *parabole* meaning "to place beside," which translates the Hebrew word *mashal*, meaning "to be like." Both the Greek and Hebrew roots suggest comparisons. In the third sermon Matthew presents comparisons between the reign of God and everyday experiences.

In addition to parables three other types of comparison are found in the Gospel: allegory, metaphor and simile. All three of these forms are closely related to parables and are also part of Jesus' methods for presenting material.

An allegory makes a comparison by substituting other images within the story itself.

Read Matthew 13:24-30; 37-39. In the space provided write the allegorical comparison.

Did you notice that the farmer is compared to the Son of Man (Matthew 13:37), the field is compared to the world, the weeds are followers of the evil one and so on?

Metaphor is a comparison between two unlikely things. The characteristics of one thing are compared and transferred to the other. An excellent example of metaphor comes from Matthew 5:13, "You are the salt of the earth."

Similes make comparisons by using the words *like* or *as*.

Read Matthew 10:16.

Notice how Jesus' instruction to his disciples is that he is sending them *like* sheep among wolves.

Exploring

Parables do not originate with Jesus. We can find parables in several Old Testament passages, for example, Isaiah 5:1-7; Ezekiel 21:5; Ezekiel 24:3; Sirach 39:2-3; Psalm 78:2. Often parables are not immediately clear; rather they tease the hearer to discover their meaning. While a parable invites the hearer into the discussion, it also requires the listener to study its obscurity (Sirach 39:3).

Some Old Testament parables are presented as riddles meant for the select few (Sirach 39:2-3). But it would be incorrect to assume that all parables could be understood only by a select group. In fact Jesus uses parables when speaking to all of his followers. For Jesus the parables were instruments of dialogue between himself and his followers. He presents parables as a way to express his point of view. He hopes that his listeners will be inspired and incorporate the message of the parable within their lives. Jesus expects opposition as a means of furthering the dialogue, and he often receives it, since some of his parables were shocking.

Discovering

When we compare parables within the Synoptic Gospels we notice that the writers take some liberty with the details and emphasis of a parable while remaining faithful to the story's message. The writers adapt the parables to the particular emphases of their Gospels.

Read Matthew 13:31-32 and Luke 13:18-19. In the space provided compare the parable and state the particular emphases made by Matthew and then by Luke. (Hint: It may be helpful to situate the parable by reading the verses prior to and following the particular passage.)

Matthew 13:31-32

Luke 13:18-19

Exploring

Both versions of the parable deal with the reign of God. Locating Matthew's parable within the sermon on the mystery of the reign of God provides a clue that he is revealing something about the magnitude of the Kingdom. Luke's version of the parable follows a story of repentance (a popular theme found in his Gospel). When believers repent of their sins they are free from infirmity and the Kingdom of God is closer at hand. Luke tells the same story, then, with a different emphasis.

Finally, both writers take great liberties with the details in the story: The mustard seed is not the smallest of seeds; it does not grow into a tree but rather into a tall bush; birds do not nest in a mustard bush but rather hide within its branches and feed on its seeds.

Discovering

We might be surprised that the introduction to Matthew's sermon on the mystery of the reign of God

begins not with a parable, but with a reference to John the Baptist. In Matthew's Gospel John plays a unique prophetic role and fulfills the Old Testament prophesy of Malachi: "Lo, I will send you/Elijah, the prophet,/Before the day of the LORD comes,/the great and terrible day" (Malachi 3:23). Therefore, if Matthew is preparing a sermon on parables, and parables are going to be the main tool Jesus will use to announce the Kingdom, it is appropriate to attest to the fact that the forerunner of the Messiah (namely John the Baptist) has indeed come. The section contrasts two prophetic voices: those prior to the coming of Jesus and that of Jesus himself.

Read Matthew 11:11-24.

Exploring

As great as John is (Matthew 11:11 claims that history has not known a man born of woman greater), he is not the Messiah. In fact, the disciples, because they share in Jesus' prophetic light, are greater than John (Matthew 11:11). Neither John's strong message of austerity nor the Zealots' violent message of "holy war" will lead people into the Kingdom. Rather Jesus' message of a renewal of faith announces the Kingdom.

Matthew informs his community that some will deny the messages of both John and Jesus. These community members are straddling the fence of faith—they deny John because of his austerity, but at the same time they deny Jesus, whom they call a glutton and drunkard for his eating and drinking with sinners. Matthew claims that "wisdom is vindicated by her works" (Matthew 11:19).

Discovering

Read Matthew 11:25-30.

Exploring

This may be the answer to Matthew's question. Wisdom lies in recognizing the relationship between Jesus and the Father. The wise person expresses in faith that "[n]o one knows the Son except the Father, and no one knows the Father except the Son and anyone to whom the Son wishes to reveal him." Here again is the heart of Matthew's message, a message that asks: Where do we find the presence, teaching and authority of God? We find it in Emmanuel, the Son of God, the Christ.

Matthew continues to warn those who reject Christ's message that they are responsible for their actions. Just as acceptance of Christ brings life, rejection brings death. We will face the consequences of our actions on the day of judgment. Although the towns of Chorazin, Bethsaida and Capernaum are geographically Jesus' home, they symbolize that even those physically close to the historical Jesus could misunderstand or reject his message. The true believer takes the message of Jesus to heart.

Discovering

Read Matthew 12.

Exploring

The chapter begins with two disputes regarding the Sabbath. In the first account, the disciples are accused of *reaping* and *preparing* food on the Sabbath, which are two of the thirty-nine actions forbidden in the rabbinic text *Sabbat*. The disciples' action is similar to action described in Deuteronomy 23:25; however, no mention of Sabbath is found in the account. The Pharisees' complaint stems from Exodus 34:21, which states that on the seventh day one should rest. Jesus presents three arguments for rebuttal. His first argument refers to a story from 1 Samuel 21:1-6 in which David and his men eat bread of the sanctuary. This account also has no mention of Sabbath. Jesus' second argument is from Leviticus 24:8, which permitted the priests to set out the bread on the Sabbath. Jesus' third and most striking argument is taken from Hosea 6:6: "For it is love that I desire, not sacrifice,/and knowledge of God rather than holocausts." This text from Hosea was also used by Matthew in 9:13, where Jesus adds, "I did not come to call the righteous but sinners."

The second Sabbath dispute centers around the healing of a man with a withered hand. According to rabbinic texts, healing is permitted on the Sabbath in extreme cases when life is in danger. From the description of the man in this account his condition appears to be a birth defect or something else that is not life threatening. Jesus responds with an argument also taken from rabbinic texts which permits animals to be removed from harmful traps on the Sabbath. Jesus' argument is that if the law allows for rescuing animals, much more should be allowed for humans.

By placing the events in both stories on the Sabbath, Matthew may be dealing with two issues of his time: the concern of Jewish-Christians with proper observation of the Sabbath day, and the theological argument that Jesus is above the Sabbath.

Scholars widely agree that Matthew's community was heavily steeped in Jewish tradition. These Jewish-Christians more than likely observed the Sabbath tradition according to the Jewish Law. References to rabbinic texts point to the fact that there was great controversy within the Jewish communities as to what constituted work on the Sabbath. For example, the Essenes held the strict interpretation that if an animal fell into a pit on the Sabbath, it was to be left to die. Other rabbinic texts allowed for more liberal interpretations. Matthew may be dealing with a pastoral situation for his community and chooses to stress the interpretation suggested by Hosea: "It is love that I desire..." (Hosea 6:6).

Matthew 12:8 says that "the Son of Man is Lord of the sabbath." Matthew places this quote after his emphasis on God desiring mercy. For Matthew the final argument is the authority of Jesus himself. His claim to be Lord of the Sabbath connects him to God, the recognized Lord of the Sabbath. The biblical and rabbinic texts are clear that God can work on the Sabbath. Further, God's work on the Sabbath is to give or take away life.

Looking Back

On Journey 11 you made the following discoveries:

- Parables are the primary teaching tool of Jesus.
- Parables were a popular teaching form, found in the Old Testament and elsewhere.
- The parable technique invites and teases hearers to discover the message beneath the obscurity of the story.
- The followers of Jesus, who share in his prophetic light, are even greater than John the Baptist.
- Jesus is the one who reveals the Father.
- Jesus, like the Father, can do the work of God on the Sabbath.

Exploring Further

Boucher, Madeleine I. *The Parables,* New Testament Message, vol. 7. Collegeville, Minn.: Michael Glazier, Inc., 1983.

Freed, Edwin D. *The New Testament: A Critical Introduction*. Belmont, Calif.: Wadsworth Publishing Company, 1991.

Journey 12

The Sermon Presented in Parables

Matthew 13 is the actual sermon on the Kingdom of God. The setting for the sermon presents Jesus in a boat by the seashore. Although the Sea of Galilee is not large, it does have numerous inlets and coves, which serve as natural amphitheaters. With the crowd listening, Jesus is ready to preach.

Discovering

Read Matthew 13.

In the space provided, list the parables presented in the chapter by writing the biblical citation (chapter and verse) plus a brief description or title for each parable.

Exploring

Compare your listing with mine.

- Matthew 13:4-9: Parable of the Seed
- Matthew 13:24-30: Parable of the Weeds
- Matthew 13:31-32: Parable of the Mustard Seed
- Matthew 13:33: Parable of the Leaven in the Bread
- Matthew 13:44: Parable of the Treasure
- Matthew 13:45-46: Parable of the Pearl
- Matthew 13:47-50: Parable of the Net

It may not be coincidental that seven parables are presented to describe the reign of God. Remember that the number seven symbolically means "to be full or have enough of" (refer to Journey 2). By presenting the sermon in seven parables, Jesus offers a full view of the reign of God.

Discovering

The seven parables, although different stories, have similar points of reference. In the space provided list the parables that you believe have the same idea.

Exploring

Check your comparisons with the ones I have listed.

- The Parable of the Seeds, the Parable of the Weeds and the Parable of the Net have a similar message of separating the good from the bad.
- The Parable of the Mustard Seed and the Parable of the Leaven in the Bread have a similar message of a small item growing and/or spreading.
- The Parable of the Treasure and the Parable of the Pearl have a similar message regarding something of value.

Discovering

The text of Matthew's sermon deals with the reign of God; therefore, each parable says something about God's Kingdom. The message is not that we await some future kingdom (heaven), but rather that God reigns and the Kingdom of God is now. God constantly reveals to humanity the existence of the Kingdom, a reign that will transform the world. Humanity responds to God's revelation by believing in the Kingdom and following the example of Christ, who reveals the Kingdom in specific ways. Each of Matthew's seven parables attests to the reign of God for the early Christian community and for all communities. The details in each of the parables are significant for the story itself. Within each parable an entire worldview is presented.

In the space provided, summarize in one or two sentences what the connected parables proclaim about the Kingdom now.

1) What is the Old Testament background?

2) How does the story fit into the life of Jesus?

Exploring

Compare your summaries with mine.
- Parables of the Seeds, Weeds and Net: Within the Kingdom there will be a judgment on the last day. The judgment will purge those who have not lived so as to bring about the Kingdom.
- The Parable of the Mustard Seed and Leaven in Bread: The Kingdom is such a powerful and dynamic force that it cannot be contained.
- The Parable of the Treasure and the Pearl: The Kingdom is of ultimate value.

3) What are the literary characteristics?

Discovering

Pheme Perkins, the biblical scholar, provides an excellent tool for studying parables. Perkins instructs students to ask five basic questions when studying parables: (1) What is the Old Testament background to the story? (2) How does the story fit into the life of Jesus? (3) What are the literary characteristics of the story? (4) What kind of everyday human situation and behavior is reflected in the story? (5) What is the theological question or statement?

Using Perkins' questions, work with Matthew's Parable of the Seed as found in Matthew 13:4-9.

4) What everyday human situation and behavior is reflected?

5) What is the theological statement?

Exploring

Compare your answers with mine.

1) What is the Old Testament background?

Concentrating on the idea of judgment and the idea that individuals will be purified, Ezekiel 39:16 speaks of the land being purified on the day of the Lord. [*Note:* A helpful tool for answering the question of Old Testament background is a concordance, a book that contains an index of words and references to biblical citations in which the word appears. Computer software programs that perform word searches in the Bible are also available.]

2) How does the story fit in the life of Jesus?

Two different approaches may be used when reflecting on how the parable fits into the life of Jesus:
(1) The sower is lavishly, perhaps foolishly, scattering good seed where it has no chance of survival; (2) the parable reflects knowledge of sowing seed in the Palestine region, which has a thin layer of topsoil.

Beginning the parable with a foolish way to sow seed, Jesus captures the attention of the audience who are shocked by the absurdity of the farmer's method of planting. If the parable reflects knowledge of farming, Jesus presents a situation that is familiar and comfortable to the audience.

3) What are the literary characteristics?

Within a few short sentences, the parable presents four outcomes for seeds. The hearer of the parable

not only knows where the seeds have fallen but is given a quick lesson as to the consequence of tossing seeds in certain locations, for example, the seeds that fall on the footpath are gobbled up by the birds.

4) What everyday human situation and behavior is reflected?

The parable is certainly about farming but also about good business practices. The question is how to obtain the best yield for the labor. The farmer is sowing good seed. Yet, the people listening to the parable understand that some of his actions are going to present a bad yield. Three-fourths of the seeds fall into areas that will not yield a good harvest. Would it not be better for the farmer to apply other techniques for sowing seed?

5) What is the theological statement?

Matthew 13:18-23 provides a theological explanation of the parable. But this is one of the few parables in which an explanation is provided. If the theological statement is presented in some generic fashion applicable to all people, it may lose its meaning. Rather, the parable's message must challenge listeners regarding their own commitment to the gospel message. Perhaps, it is best to answer the theological statement with a series of questions:

- Where has the word of God fallen within my lifetime?
- In what specific manner have I harvested good seed?
- What preparations must I make in order to hear the word of God and believe it?

For me, the theological statement can be reduced to two significant questions: What particular value found in the gospel do I wish to express in my daily life? What specific action have I performed within the past twenty-four hours that demonstrates the specific gospel value?

Looking Back

In Journey 12 you made the following discoveries:

- The sermon on the mystery of the reign of God is presented in seven parables.
- Each parable presents an entire worldview.
- The reign of God is a dynamic force, is of ultimate value and is a place where individuals will be purified.
- Through working with Pheme Perkins' five questions for studying parables, one may gain greater insight into the story and its meaning for one's life.

Exploring Further

Jeremias, Joachim. *The Parables of Jesus*. New York: Scribner, 1963.

Perkins, Pheme. *Hearing The Parables of Jesus*. New York: Paulist Press, 1981.

Journey 13

A Change in Perspective

A number of years ago, when I first heard the family referred to as the "domestic Church," I had trouble grasping the concept. I had never thought of the family that way. I also realized I had never thought of the Church that way—as a family rather than as buildings or a large institution. I had to make some changes in the way I thought about Church. Matthew, in his preliminary chapters to his sermon on Church, may be changing his readers' perceptions about who actually makes up the membership of the Church.

Discovering

We can begin to explore Matthew's preliminary presentation of Church through a study of two characters: Peter and the Canaanite woman.

In the space provided, briefly paraphrase the following verses. After reflecting on each verse, write a sentence that describes the image of Peter presented in these passages.

Matthew 14:28-33

Matthew 15:15

Matthew 16:13-22

Matthew 17:1-8

Matthew 17:24-27

Image of Peter:

Exploring

Compare your summaries with mine.

- Matthew 14:28-33: In the walking on water story, Peter loses faith in Jesus and begins to sink in the waters.
- Matthew 15:15: Peter asks for an explanation of the parable and Jesus appears disgruntled that the disciples still don't understand his teaching.
- Matthew 16:13-22: Jesus declares that Peter is the rock on which the Church is to be built. In the next line, though, Jesus refers to Peter as a Satan.
- Matthew 17:1-8: Peter, after witnessing the transfiguration of Jesus, wants to build three booths in God's honor.
- Matthew 17:24-27: Peter professes that Jesus pays taxes; Jesus questions Peter on the matter of taxation and then instructs Peter to pay the taxes for both of them after retrieving the money from the mouth of a fish.

- Image of Peter: He appears to be an impetuous character who is always making rash and inappropriate statements.
- We may have an image of Peter as an original follower of Christ, the head of apostles and eventually the first pope. Matthew's image of Peter may be a device for instructing Church members how not to behave.

Reread Matthew 14:13-33.

Two major events are presented in Chapter 14: feeding the multitude and walking on water. The accounts refer to two significant Old Testament accounts found in Exodus: crossing the Red Sea/Sea of Reeds (Exodus 14:10ff.) and manna in the desert (Exodus 16:4ff.). The account portrays Jesus doing what God does: feeding and liberating. Again, Matthew reminds his community that the actions of Jesus are the actions of God. The two accounts also represent the liberation and life of members of the Church through Baptism and Eucharist, a reminder that the actions of the Church are the actions of Christ.

Peter's near drowning is reminiscent of numerous Old Testament accounts of God saving his people from drowning. For example, Psalm 107 says, "In their distress they cried to the LORD,/who brought them out of their peril,/Hushed the storm to a murmur;/the waves of the sea were stilled" (Psalm 107:28-29).

Peter, representing all disciples, is depicted in this scene as a man of little faith. Even after witnessing all that Jesus has done, he falters. Once safe inside the boat, he joins the others in proclaiming Jesus as the Son of God. He represents the blend of strong and weak faith found in all of us.

Discovering

Reread Matthew 15:10-20.

Peter requests an explanation for something that he should have understood. If he, a good Jew, lacks understanding of the Leviticus rules on cleanliness, we might assume that Matthew's community also lacks understanding of the new law given by Christ. We can find a sign of hope in Acts 10—11, where Peter truly understands and preaches about cleanliness and the law.

Discovering

Reread Matthew 16:13-23.

In the first half of the account Peter attests to the fact that Jesus is the Messiah, the Son of the Living God. For this acclamation he is given authority as leader of the Church. The difficulty is that Peter immediately misunderstands the nature of authority when he attempts to dissuade Jesus from his path in life. Peter expected Christ to be a political, ruling messiah, one who would free Israel from Roman domination. He had to learn that Jesus was a different kind of messiah. Like Peter, the members of the Church need to learn to let go of their expectations and accept Jesus as a servant messiah.

Discovering

Reread Matthew 17.

This chapter presents two images of Peter. In the first image Peter misunderstands the significance of the transfiguration and wants to build altars. He recognizes the reverence in the scene but he wants to keep these three figures removed from reality. He does not see that Jesus is again on a mountain as the new Moses. Rather than anticipating the coming of the Lord, of which the transfiguration is only a preview, Peter wants to undertake a building project.

The conversation between Jesus and Peter about taxes reveals several things about the Church. Peter speaks (correctly) for Jesus to those who question his behavior. This shows the closeness between Peter and Jesus, as does Jesus finding the money to pay the tax for both of them. After a long explanation of why his followers do not need to pay taxes, Jesus still tells Peter to pay the tax in order not to cause scandal, which is a major point in the actual sermon on the Church.

Discovering

We can also learn something about the Church from the story of the Canaanite woman.

Read Matthew 15:21-28. In the space provided write one or two sentences that explain the lesson it contains about the Church.

Exploring

Here is my summary of the lesson of Matthew 15:21-28. The Canaanite woman is a model of faith and persistent prayer. She kneels before Jesus saying, "Lord, help me."

Jesus responds by saying, "Woman, great is your faith."

The image of a Gentile woman coming to Jesus as a person of faith must have been difficult for Matthew's community to accept. Relations between Jewish-Christians and Gentiles were strained in the community. By telling the story of this woman, Matthew reminds his community that all are brought to God through Jesus. It is the role of the Church to invite all to partake of life in Christ.

Looking Back

On Journey 13 you made the following discoveries:

- The Church is primarily the people of God, not a building or institution.
- Models for the Church can be found in Peter and the Canaanite woman.
- Jesus, like God, performs works of liberation.
- Jesus' works of life and liberation can be witnessed in the Church through Baptism and Eucharist.

Exploring Further

Apicella, Raymond. *Journeys Into Mark: 16 Lessons of Exploration and Discovery.* Cincinnati, Ohio: St. Anthony Messenger Press, 1990.

Journey 14

The Sermon on the Church

Every time I meet my five-year-old neighbor, she greets me with, "You know what?" My simple response of "What?" permits her to relate some fascinating event of her day. With a flurry of hand movements and facial expressions she entertains me with stories of how my dog chased the cat, how her finger-paints spilled on her dress or how the repairman had to fix the washing machine. Each story ends with a simple lesson that is often profound: "If you would introduce your dog to the cat, she wouldn't be so upset and then they would be friends!" I look forward to my conversations with Leslie Ann; she challenges me to see life's situations in a different light.

Discovering

Matthew, in his sermon on the Church, challenges his community to see Church in a different light. To those who have a confused and complicated view of the Church, Matthew puts the question, "Do you know what Church is?"

Read Matthew 18.

In the space provided, write Matthew's characteristics for the Church. Try to list seven characteristics.

To be Church, we must:

1)

2)

3)

4)

5)

6)

7)

Exploring

Compare your list of Church characteristics with mine.

To be Church, we must:

1) be childlike (18:1-4);

2) welcome the weak (18:5);

3) avoid scandal (18:6-9);

4) evangelize (18:10-14);

5) correct one another (18:15-18);

6) pray (18:19-20);

7) forgive (18:21-34).

The instruction to be childlike is connected to the first Beatitude found in Matthew 5, "Blessed are the poor in spirit." Children in the first century were considered pieces of property without any rights. They were utterly defenseless in the eyes of society and totally dependent upon others for their needs. In telling his followers to be childlike, then, Jesus instructs the Church to be utterly defenseless and trust only in the God who gives all things. Church members must be humble as Jesus humbled himself even to death. The childlike understand the glorious revelation of the Kingdom that has been hidden from the learned and the clever (Matthew 11:25).

Discovering

Matthew's Jesus fulfills Isaiah's prophecy: "Yet it was our infirmities that he bore,/our sufferings that he endured" (Isaiah 53:4). Matthew restates this prophecy after saying that Jesus exorcised and healed many throughout the night (Matthew 8:16-17).

Read the following healing stories. In the space provided write a statement that explains the motivation for Jesus' healing.

Matthew 9:27-29

Matthew 9:35-36

Matthew 14:14

Matthew 15:22

Exploring

Compare your list with mine.

- Matthew 9:27-29: He responds to the cries of the two men, "Son of David have pity on us!"
- Matthew 9:35-36: He cures all kinds of illnesses because his heart was moved to pity.
- Matthew 14:14: His heart was moved to pity so he cured the crowd.
- Matthew 15:22: He responds to the Canaanite woman's plea, "Have pity on me, Lord, Son of David."

We see from these examples that Jesus healed because he had pity on people. This kind of pity, which demonstrates mercy and compassion, relates to the Beatitude, "Blessed are the merciful." To live this Beatitude, Church members are to treat all others as brothers and sisters. Those who have mercy want all people to be whole.

Exploring

The next two characteristics, avoiding scandal and evangelizing, hint at two choices the Church has in dealing with its members. The Church can be either an instrument of sin, which brings death, or an instrument of redemption, which brings life. Jesus' example is always to avoid scandal (recall the discussion of taxes in Journey 13, Matthew 17:27).

Jubilation and rejoicing after finding the lost is a theme Matthew shares with Luke. Shock is the first reaction to the story. The people hearing the story are familiar with shepherding. Their immediate reaction is that only a foolish shepherd would leave what he has (the ninety-nine) to seek what he does not have (the one sheep). When he returned to the flock most likely all the sheep would have scattered. Jesus' point in telling the parable is not to describe good shepherding practices. He is rather telling Church members that their primary concern should be for the weak. Jesus himself set an example when he had pity for the people who were "troubled and abandoned, like sheep without a shepherd" (Matthew 9:36).

Exploring

The admonition regarding fraternal correction is the second occasion in which Matthew uses the word *church* (*ekklesia* in Greek). Out of all four Gospels this Greek term is found only in Matthew 16:18 and Matthew 18:17. The first refers to Peter as the rock on which the

Church will be built. In the second reference, part of the sermon on the Church, the power of binding and loosing, which was given to Peter, is now given to the Church.

The procedure the Church is to use for fraternal correction is adapted from two Old Testament passages. Leviticus 19:17 teaches that one should not hate others but rather reason with them. Deuteronomy 19:15 says two or three witnesses are required to sustain a charge against another. Both passages deal with procedures for dealing with criminals; Matthew adapts them to apply to dealing with straying Church members.

The teaching on prayer is also rooted in ancient Hebrew texts. The Israelites believed that when one studies the Law of God with another, the words of the Law pass between them, which allows the presence of God to abide between them. Matthew again adapts a juridical statement from the Law to encourage communal prayer.

Discovering

The final characteristic, forgiveness, is presented in parable form. The story of the merciless official provides an opportunity to practice another way of dealing with parables. Megan McKenna suggests different questions than the five discussed in Journey 12. Her three questions provide an excellent opportunity to adapt the primary message of the parable into one's own life.

After rereading Matthew 18:21-33, answer the following questions.

1) What in the parable rings true to you?

2) What in the parable disturbs you?

3) What are you going to do about the disturbance?

Exploring

Compare your answers to mine. Remember that McKenna's questions are personal, so no two responses need to be alike.

1) What in the parable rings true to you?

The master is moved with pity, which affirms my belief that God is merciful. Unfortunately, at times I do not demonstrate that pity and instead seek retaliation, hatred and injustice.

2) What in the parable disturbs you?

The fact that I am more like the official than the master. What is more disturbing is that behavior similar

to the official's appears to be the common behavior of our society.

3) What are you going to do about the disturbance?

Specifically, I need to work for justice in my workplace and my community. I must become an advocate for those who are weak.

Exploring

Each of the seven characteristics of the Church deal with relationships. To be Church is to be in relationship with others in building the Kingdom of God. This relationship is best expressed in the Roman Catholic liturgy, where we pray as a community. The prayers of the liturgy most often use the first person plural (we, our, us), expressing our unity with one another before God.

Looking Back

In Journey 14 you made the following discoveries:

- Matthew's sermon on the Church presents seven characteristics.
- These characteristics of the Church emphasize our communal relationship.
- Three questions paraphrased from Megan McKenna offer us another method of applying the parables to our lives.

Exploring Further

McKenna, Megan. *Parables: The Arrows of God.* Maryknoll, N.Y.: Orbis Books, 1994.

Journey 15

Apocalyptic Writing: Sermon on the Endtime

Matthew's sermon on the endtime provides an opportunity to investigate the literary form known as apocalyptic. It was prevalent during the four hundred years from the Maccabean uprising (167 B.C.E.) to the final destruction of Jerusalem (135 C.E.). The best examples of this literary style are the Book of Daniel in the Old Testament and the Book of Revelation in the New Testament.

Apocalyptic writing offers a sign of hope for dealing with some underlying problem. During times of persecution apocalyptic literature was used to encourage people to rely on God despite the horrific events of the day. This comfort is presented as having been originally revealed as a secret to a servant of God who in turn will reveal the secret to the world at the appropriate time. Although the revelation is ongoing, the message applies to another world, or to this world following a transformation. Because of its otherworldliness the message must be interpreted by a spiritual guide (often an angel) who can unravel the ancient secret. The literary form unfolds, in highly symbolic language, the inevitable judgment on the world, the destruction of the wicked and the transformation of the cosmic universe.

Discovering

The apocalyptic writing style influenced the Gospel writers, and each presents Jesus as the ultimate apocalyptic figure. Jesus as the Son of Man will come at the end of human history to judge the living and the dead. The end of human history will mark the beginning of the fulfillment of God's Kingdom.

Reread Matthew 19—23. While reading the section, pay special attention to the subtitles listed in your Bible, especially "The Rich Young Man" (9:16-30), "The Workers in the Vineyard" (20:1-16), "The Cursing of the Fig Tree" (21:18-22) and "The Parable of the Wedding Feast" (22:1-14). (Note: Wording may vary; the subtitles given here are taken from the *New American Bible with Revised New Testament*.)

Exploring

The *New American Bible* divides this preliminary narrative to the sermon on the endtime into nineteen sections. Some of the topics have been discussed in previous Journeys. The four subtitles selected here were chosen because many people find them difficult to understand. We need to look at them from an apocalyptic point of view to understand why, for example, the fig tree is cursed or the wedding guest is thrown out for not being properly dressed. Remember that apocalyptic literature has to do with the endtime. Ask, then, what each story says about the end of human history.

Discovering

In the space provided, write one or two sentences that describe what you believe is the endtime message for each of the four stories.

The Rich Young Man (Matthew 19:16-30)

The Workers in the Vineyard (Matthew 20:1-16)

The Cursing of the Fig Tree (Matthew 21:18-22)

The Parable of the Wedding Feast (Matthew 22:1-14)

Exploring

Compare your answers with mine.

- The Rich Young Man (Matthew 19:16-30): In the end, possessions and material things won't matter. What will matter is our relationship with God and with other people.
- The Workers in the Vineyard (Matthew 20:1-16): In the end, if the last shall be first and the first last, we will have to give an accounting of our willingness to serve all humanity with the kind of generosity shown by God.
- The Cursing of the Fig Tree (Matthew 21:18-22): In the end, God will judge us according to the "fruit" of faith (actions).
- The Parable of the Wedding Feast (Matthew 22:1-14): In the end, the Son of Man will come quickly; we must be ready at any time.

The story of the rich young man appears to conflict with Old Testament teachings that said wealth was a blessing from God (see Deuteronomy 28:1-14). This may be why the disciples are overwhelmed and exclaim, "Who then can be saved?" The man has also openly admitted that he has kept all the commandments, including the commandment to love one's neighbor.

The key to understanding the story may lie in the statement, "If you wish to be perfect...." Again, *perfect* here means wholeness and complete dedication to God. It is a call to seek justice in all things and to do God's will completely. The man is being asked to give everything and follow Christ on a journey that will bring him to the cross. The man in the story cannot make this journey. Instead of possessing riches, his riches may have possessed him.

The vineyard is often a symbol for Israel; in this story it becomes a symbol for the Kingdom. The problem is the apparent unfair labor practices. The workers receive the same salary for different hours of work. But the story cannot be viewed from a human perspective, which gives great honor to the wealthy, the elite and even those who work hard. Rather the story must be viewed from the perspective of Jesus, who has come for the marginal: the tax collectors, sinners and those who are disabled. To understand the Kingdom of God, we must reverse our ideas of position and status: Those who think they are insiders are cast out, while those who have been led to believe that they are outsiders are treated generously.

Jesus' bizarre behavior in cursing the fig tree causes great difficulty if we view it literally. But if we look at it in its context we see that it is sandwiched between the story of the cleansing of the Temple and the story about Jesus' authority. This placement suggests that the cursing of the fig tree may be saying something about leadership more than anything else.

Throughout this Gospel Matthew is rather harsh with the leadership of Israel. His harshness is justified: the leaders appointed by God to shepherd the people have become hypocrites. Matthew 23 details Jesus' difficulty with Israel's leadership. The leaders, symbolized by the tree, have lost faith. Because of their failure, their leadership will be transferred to the twelve apostles (the new twelve tribes of Israel)—provided they have faith.

Matthew begins the story of the wedding banquet with the popular comparison of the reign of God to a wedding feast. This image portrays God sitting at table with the people in a culture where eating together carried great significance. Jesus is often portrayed eating with "sinners and tax collectors," revealing that the outcast and the poor will have a place at the table in the Kingdom. The ultimate banquet image of God's reign is of course the Last Supper (Matthew 26:26-30).

The parable here presents a rejection of people who want to sit at table with the Messiah but are unwilling to make an effort. The first group of invited guests are like those who refused to hear the prophets. The second group becomes more hostile, insulting and killing the servants; this is similar to the treatment given to John the Baptist. The third group is destroyed by the king's army, which may hint at some final destruction. The refusal of the first group leads to the invitation being extended to all—even the tax collectors and sinners. Note that the invitation is extended not merely because these people are sinners. Rather, it is their readiness to hear the invitation and to serve the Kingdom of God.

The point of this preliminary narrative is summarized in the commandment presented in Matthew 22:34-40.

Reread Matthew 22:34-40. In the space provided write the key points presented in the passage.

Exploring

Compare your key points with those presented below.

- A lawyer attempts to entrap Jesus.
- The lawyer calls Jesus "teacher."
- Jesus presents the two commandments as the foundation for the whole Law and the prophets.

The lawyer asks a question in a typical attempt to trap Jesus. More than likely, he is a scribe who has been trained in the Torah; therefore, he knows the Law. Jesus responds from the Torah with the Shema (Deuteronomy 6:4-5) and adds the love of neighbor found in Leviticus 19:18.

"Teacher" is not a popular title for Jesus in Matthew's Gospel; it is primarily used by those who have difficulty believing in Jesus. Seven of the nine passages in which Jesus is called "teacher" are spoken by Pharisees, Sadducees or their disciples—all those who refuse to see Jesus as the Messiah. Matthew prefers the title "Son of Man," which he uses approximately thirty times. The Son of Man is an apocalyptic figure, that is, the suffering servant of God who will come on the last day to judge the living and the dead.

Presenting the two commandments as the foundation for the whole Law and the prophets is a popular theme in Matthew's Gospel.

Discovering

Reread Matthew 5:17; 7:12; 11:13.

For Matthew, God's whole revelation is presented in the law of love. This law binds believers to God and frees them from legalism and unnecessary restraints.

Looking Back

On Journey 15 you made the following discoveries:

- Apocalyptic literature was a popular form of writing during the time of the Gospel writers.
- Apocalyptic literature provides a message of hope during times of great persecution.
- The narrative in Matthew 19—23 that prepares for the sermon on the endtime is filled with stories that provide a glimpse of the endtime.
- The commandment of love fulfills the Law and the prophets.

Exploring Further

Collins, John. *The Apocalyptic Imagination: An Introduction to the Jewish Matrix of Christianity.* New York: The Crossroad Publishing Company, 1992.

Spivey, Robert A. and D. Moody Smith. *Anatomy of the New Testament: A Guide to Its Structure and Meaning,* 3rd ed. New York: Macmillan, 1982.

Journey 16
The Endtime Sermon

Many people believe that the world is coming to an end, although when and how are much debated. From a biblical perspective it is true that the world will end, but we need to see this from a theological rather than historical perspective. Within the context of the Bible, the end is a dramatic transformation of the world so that a new world (the new Jerusalem) will be reborn. This transformation marks the end of the apocalyptic time when the Son of Man will come to judge all humanity.

The study of the endtime is referred to as eschatology; the impact of apocalyptic eschatology greatly influences New Testament accounts. The passion, death and resurrection of Jesus, as well as the political and social unrest of the times, all added to a profound awareness of the eschaton. Matthew's community witnessed the destruction of the Temple (approximately 70 C.E.), the martyrdom of some eyewitnesses (Peter's death is placed around 68 C.E.) and the chaos between Christians and Jews over the synagogues. All this upheaval led to a sense that the end was near.

Discovering

Reread Matthew's endtime sermon (Matthew 24—26) in this context of the endtime being near. In the space provided, write the major ideas regarding the endtime that Matthew presents to his community.

Exploring

Compare your listing with mine.

- There will be terrible destruction.
- There will be false prophets; many will claim to be the Messiah.
- The believer must be watchful.
- The Son of Man will come in glory and dispatch his angels with a mighty trumpet blast.
- The good and the evil will be separated and judged.

Exploring

The setting (the Garden of Olives) for the prediction of destruction is apocalyptic (see Zechariah 14:1-9). In the first stage of the endtime, wars between nations and natural disasters will take place. The important thing about this apocalyptic image is not a reference to any particular war or disaster, but rather that these events are all part of God's plan. The true believer realizes that these are the "early stages of birth pangs," that is, the period of chaos and confusion that precedes the coming of the Messiah.

Along with destruction from without (warring nations and natural disasters), a more disturbing destruction will come from within the community. Some followers will become false prophets and "mislead many"—another example of Matthew's difficulty with those who scandalize others. The corrosion of the community from within (through false prophesy and apostasy) will lead to persecution and strife from the many who falter and hate one another. This echoes the Beatitude "Blessed are you when they insult you and persecute you...."

One technique of apocalyptic writers is to place the account of a past historical event on the lips of a messenger in the form of a future prediction. For example, at the time Matthew is writing, the Temple had been destroyed and Jerusalem razed. Matthew 24:15-28 describes the endtime in terms of the reactions people had to the destruction of Jerusalem.

The reinterpretation of these events with a view to the endtime is further seen as a fulfillment of the Old Testament apocalyptic writer Daniel. At the time of Daniel, around 167 B.C.E., Antiochus IV set up a false god in the Temple. This is the abomination to which Daniel refers (Daniel 11:31). In 40 C.E. the Roman emperor Caligula attempted to place a statue of himself inside the Jewish Temple.

Matthew draws on these past experiences to create an image for his community of the abomination to come with the endtime. Just as individuals reacted during the historical situations (fleeing immediately, fleeing with children, fleeing on the sabbath), people will react to the final judgment time.

With the coming of the Son of Man, the believer must be vigilant: "For you do not know on which day your Lord will come" (Matthew 24:42). Similar to today, it appears that some members of the community were interested in the exact time when the end will occur. Matthew may be warning his community, and us, that the exact day and hour is not ours to know (see Matthew 24:36). The theme of vigilance is played out in two parables: the ten virgins (Matthew 25:1-13) and the talents (Matthew 25:14-30).

Discovering

Journey 15 explained that the Son of Man is an apocalyptic figure, appointed by God, to judge the living and the dead.

Read Daniel 7:13.

Exploring

The same image of the Son of Man riding a cloud is now applied to Jesus in Matthew's depiction of the endtime. Closely linked with the coming of the Son of Man is the theme of judgment. The judgment is toward all, Jew and Gentile, seen in the image of angels being dispatched with a mighty trumpet blast to assemble all peoples from the four winds.

The judgment scene in Matthew's Gospel is the most detailed and perhaps the most frightening (Matthew 25:31-46). It is a culmination of the five sermons with the simple message that while we wait for the Son of Man to come to judge the world, we are to recognize the Son of Man in everyone we encounter. This is actually a judgment of mercy based on the Beatitudes; it rewards those who are poor in spirit, judging them by their willingness to give up all for the Kingdom—even one's life.

Discovering

The final judgment scene provides an excellent opportunity for personal reflection. The questions listed here are guidelines for personal examination of conscience. The importance of the exercise is to recommit your life to Christ; do not use it to beat yourself for past decisions, behaviors or life-styles.

1) What specific actions within my life fulfill the conditions set forth in the judgment scene? When did I clothe the naked, feed the hungry, comfort the ill or those in prison?

2) In order to fulfill the conditions of the judgment scene, what specific actions do I plan on undertaking within the next month, the next six months and the next year?

Looking Back

In Journey 16 you made the following discoveries:

- Matthew's final sermon on the endtime is an example of eschatology.
- The sermon unfolds the ideas of destruction, watchfulness, Son of Man and judgment.
- Apocalyptic literature uses a technique of creating a future prediction from a past significant event.
- The final judgment will be based on how well we serve others while waiting for the coming of the Lord.

Exploring Further

Meier, John P. *Matthew*. New Testament Message, vol. 3. Collegeville, Minn.: Michael Glazier, Inc., 1980.

Senior, Donald, ed. "Biblical Update: The End of the World." *The Bible Today*, Vol. 30, No. 1. January 1992.

Journey 17

The Passion, Death and Resurrection: The Heart of the Sermons

One difficulty we often have today when we try to understand the Scriptures is that we believe we know the story without *really* knowing the story. The wide availability of Bibles, the daily and weekly reading of the Gospels at liturgical services, numerous opportunities for Bible study (all good in themselves) may create a false assurance that people are biblically literate. Hearing the words so often may cause us to skip to the end of the story or daydream about another story. We need to develop "biblical ears," the ability to hear not only the story but all the details and nuances of the story. With "biblical ears" we hear the message in a new way and gain new insights.

Discovering

One way to hear the story with "biblical ears" is to place yourself within the passage. This reflective exercise allows you to sharpen your senses and hear the story anew.

Read through the entire exercise in order to become comfortable with the steps presented. Then, after the initial reading, do the exercise.

1) Slowly read Matthew 26—27. While reading try to remember the general sequence of events.

2) Place yourself in a relaxed position.

3) Leave your Bible on your lap. Use your imagination to paraphrase Matthew 26—27.

4) As you recall the story place yourself within the passage. Do not hover over the scene. Find a concrete location from which you can observe all the action.

5) Retell the conversations that occur within the story. Imagine the sounds of people's voices, the looks on their faces and the way others react to what they say.

6) Concentrate especially on the main characters within the story.

7) When you have retold the story in your imagination, in the space provided write any new insights you gained from the exercise. Record the names of the main characters with a brief description of the roles they played within the story and Jesus' reaction to their roles.

New insights I gained...:

Main characters:

Exploring

Compare your listing of main characters with mine.

1) Caiaphas (and the chief priests and elders)

2) woman who anoints Jesus' feet

3) the disciples, especially Judas and Peter

4) Pilate

5) Barabbas

6) Simon the Cyrenian

7) the centurion

8) the women: Mary Magdalene, Mary the mother of James and Joseph, and the mother of Zebedee's sons

9) Joseph of Arimathea

Through a study of these main characters we hope to discover new insights into the passion narrative.

1) The setting for killing Jesus is the Passover—the celebration of the liberation of the Israelites from Egyptian slavery. This is ironic—the officials (Caiaphas, the chief priests and the elders) who are the main celebrants of the Passover feast are plotting to kill the one who brings total liberation.

Matthew 26:57-68 tells us the chief priests and elders have obtained false witnesses against Jesus. Matthew points out that two witnesses come forth—the number required by Jewish Law (Deuteronomy 17:6).

The accusation is the ability to destroy the Temple—a statement of blasphemy. Jesus does not defend this statement but rather predicts the coming of the Son of Man. Jesus' response to the accusation provides the priests and elders with the necessary proof to put him to death.

We have already commented that Jesus represents life and freedom in opposition to the plotting of the chief priests and elders. Jesus, who is life and truth, is brought before those who represent death and lies. He responds to their accusation by portraying himself as the apocalyptic figure who will replace the Temple with the new Jerusalem designed by God.

2) The woman who anoints Jesus' feet provides a contrast to the harsh treatment of the chief priests and elders. The officials spit at and slap Jesus while she anoints his body with precious perfume. She recognizes Jesus as the Son of Man and treats him with profound reverence and respect. Only Jesus knows her purpose—to prepare his body for burial.

3) Although the term *disciple* is found several times within the passion narrative, two citations are especially significant. The disciples criticize the woman for what they believe is extravagance and at the arrest of Jesus the disciples desert him and flee. The major contrast in discipleship is between Judas and Peter. Both find it difficult to witness to Jesus as the Son of Man: Judas betrays Jesus; Peter denies him.

Judas assumes the role of the betrayer—and more importantly the betrayer of innocent blood. That he betrayed an innocent man is confirmed by the officials using the money to buy a potter's field. The question of Judas' repentance has baffled many scholars. Is his return of the money a sign of repentance? If so, how do we reconcile the act of returning the money, Judas' subsequent suicide and Jesus' statement, "...woe to that man by whom the Son of Man is betrayed" (Matthew 26:24)? Judas had a choice: the choice to follow Christ and also the choice to ask for forgiveness.

The same choice was given to Peter (although Peter's denial does not result in Jesus' death as does Judas' betrayal). The fact that Peter denies Jesus three times appears to be authentic. All four Gospel writers place this event within their passion narratives. Peter seeks forgiveness, portrayed by his going out and weeping bitterly. He may be an example for the Christian community of the need to seek forgiveness.

Peter's character is also in direct contrast to the character of Jesus. Peter is unable to remain faithful to his commitment to discipleship and is a coward when faced with opposition. Jesus, on the other hand, is the model for all disciples: he is willing to face all of life's challenges and is faithful to the end.

4) Pilate is a tormented leader trying to appease both the crowd and his conscience. He realizes Jesus is innocent but fears the crowd. The fact that Jesus is innocent is confirmed by Pilate's wife's dream. Recall that we saw messages in dreams in Matthew's infancy narrative. This was an acceptable source of truth at that time. Despite knowing that Jesus is innocent, Pilate presides on the bench (judgment seat) to condemn Jesus. The believer knows the foolishness of the scene—Jesus as the Son of Man will preside over all humanity and pronounce the true judgment.

5) The comparison between Barabbas and Jesus is rather obvious. Barabbas is declared a "notorious prisoner," yet we do not know what crimes he committed to be labeled so dangerous. We know Jesus is innocent of any crime. The one who is innocent and should be set free (Jesus) is held so that the one who is guilty (Barabbas) is liberated. The climax between these contrasting characters is demonstrated by the crowd screaming for the release of Barabbas and the crucifixion of Jesus. The crowd is referred to as "all the people"—a reference that

has caused much debate among biblical scholars. It may be a reminder that we must accept the consequence of our actions, to be revealed at the time of judgment by the Son of Man.

6) The Synoptic writers refer to Simon the Cyrenian as the one who helps Jesus carry his cross. He may be a historical figure (Mark 15:21 refers to his sons). Whether the Romans permitted a person to help a condemned man carry his cross is somewhat debated. The most widely accepted argument is that Simon was permitted to assist Jesus who had been weakened by the scourging. If Simon is indeed the father of Alexander and Rufus, he may be an eyewitness to Jesus' passion.

7) Three responses to Jesus' death are portrayed in Matthew's Gospel. The centurion (a Gentile and nonbeliever) makes a profound expression of faith by stating, "Truly this was the Son of God!" What appears to be absurd—the death of Jesus—becomes a conversion experience as the centurion gains insight into Jesus' true identity as the Son of God. He believes that Jesus is the Messiah even though he previously was not a follower.

8) The centurion may be in contrast to the many women who were present "looking on from a distance." Although the Gospel claims that they followed to minister to Jesus' needs, it is impossible to assist an individual from afar. The women, who are followers, are too far away to be witnesses. The twelve, Jesus' closest followers throughout his ministry, have already fled.

9) Apparently only one disciple remains with Jesus until the end—Joseph of Arimathea. A wealthy man, he stands in contrast to the rich young man of Matthew 19. A faithful disciple, he is in contrast to the women who stand at a distance and to the twelve apostles who have fled. He becomes a model of Christian discipleship for the members of Matthew's community and all Christian communities.

Discovering

The Journey began with a reflective exercise in which you placed yourself within the passage. In the following exercise, try to assume the roles of each of the characters. In the space provided, write your reflections on assuming the role of each character.

1) Caiaphas

2) the woman who anoints Jesus' feet

3) the disciples, especially Judas and Peter

4) Pilate

7) the centurion

5) Barabbas

8) the women: Mary Magdalene, Mary the mother of James and Joseph, and the mother of Zebedee's sons

6) Simon the Cyrenian

9) Joseph of Arimathea.

Looking Back

On Journey 17, you made the following discoveries:

- Placing yourself within a Scripture passage as an observer provides insights into the biblical message.
- Assuming the roles of the main characters in a scene enables you to gain insight into a biblical passage.
- The major characters within the Passion provide contrasts to one another and to Jesus.
- In all of the passages, only three characters (the woman who anoints Jesus, the centurion and Joseph of Arimathea) truly understand the role of Christian discipleship.

Exploring Further

Brown, Raymond E. *The Death of the Messiah*, vols. 1 and 2. New York: Doubleday, 1994.

Journey 18

The Resurrection and Commissioning

Journey 17 provided two reflective exercises for gaining insight into scriptural passages. Another approach is to compare an account with the other Gospel writers. Recall that Matthew's Gospel is one of the Synoptic accounts, that is, it can be laid side-by-side with Mark and Luke. Although the accounts are not exactly the same, there is considerable similarity. By studying the similarities and differences among the Synoptic writers, we discover new things about each writer's purposes.

Discovering

Each of the Synoptic writers (and John as well) follow the passion and death narratives with scenes of the women at the tomb. Read each of the Synoptic accounts of the women at the tomb and then complete the chart with the appropriate information.

Read Matthew 28:1-8; Mark 16:1-8; Luke 24:1-8.

Time

Matthew

Mark

Luke

Characters

Matthew

Mark

Luke

Reason for Visit

Matthew

Mark

Mark

Luke

Luke

Visual Appearances

Matthew

Reaction

Matthew

Mark

Mark

Luke

Luke

Conversation

Matthew

Exploring

Compare your answers with mine.

Time

- Matthew: after the Sabbath as the first day of the week was dawning
- Mark: very early, just after sunrise on the first day of the week
- Luke: first day of the week at dawn

Characters

- Matthew: Mary Magdalene and the other Mary
- Mark: Mary Magdalene, Mary the mother of James, Salome
- Luke: Mary Magdalene, Joanna, Mary the mother of James

Reason for Visit

- Matthew: to inspect the tomb
- Mark: to anoint Jesus
- Luke: bringing prepared spices (to anoint Jesus)

Visual Appearances

- Matthew: a mighty earthquake, an angel descending, stone rolled back and angel sitting on stone
- Mark: huge stone rolled back, young man sitting inside of tomb on right
- Luke: stone rolled back and two men standing inside tomb

Conversation

- Matthew: angel says not to be frightened, Jesus has been raised, go and tell the disciples, you will see Jesus in Galilee
- Mark: young man says not to be amazed, Jesus has been raised up, go tell disciples and Peter that Jesus is going ahead of them to Galilee
- Luke: two men ask why they are looking for the living among the dead; Jesus has been raised up

Reaction

- Matthew: hurried away from the tomb half-overjoyed, half-fearful, and ran to tell the disciples
- Mark: fled bewildered and trembling

- Luke: women remember the words of Jesus

Exploring

First we will compare the similarities among these accounts. The timing of the event and the message delivered are similar in all three accounts. It is no accident that each writer places the time of the event at dawn of the first day of the week. Those attuned to biblical detail will realize that the beginning of the resurrection event corresponds with the beginning of creation itself (Genesis 1). Just as God began the world with light, it is at first light that the new world created by the passion, death and resurrection of the Son of God is being created. Every writer emphasizes that this marks a new beginning—the beginning of the Christian era.

All three Gospels record the message to announce the new era. The women are told not to be afraid, that Jesus has risen and gone to Galilee. This is the central faith proclamation of the Christian community: Jesus Christ is risen from the dead. There is no need to fear—death has been overcome.

No one actually sees the resurrection take place; the resurrection cannot be proven historically or scientifically. From a purely historical perspective the body could have been stolen. A scientific explanation would suggest resuscitation or reanimation. Resurrection assumes that the resurrected person will never die again.

The gospel message is not history or science, but faith; we witness to the experience of God alive in our lives. The women recall that Jesus predicted his passion and death, as well as other events throughout his ministry. These events occurred just as Jesus said; there is no reason to doubt his resurrection or his going ahead to Galilee since he predicted all of this in Matthew 26:32.

Jesus returns to Galilee, where he had begun his ministry and called his disciples. He is not in the place of death (the tomb or Jerusalem) but in the place of life, now symbolically associated with Galilee. Galilee is also associated with the Gentiles, suggesting the expansion of his mission to all the world.

Exploring

Differences in the Synoptic accounts are purposely placed by the writer to highlight specific points for community instruction as well as to recall overall Gospel themes. For example, Luke places two men inside the tomb, as evangelization is always undertaken by a pair of disciples (see Luke 10:1 where Jesus sends the disciples out two by two). Mark places in the tomb a young man in dazzling white clothing, recalling both the transfigured Christ (Mark 9:1-10) and the young man fleeing in the garden (Mark 14:51).

Matthew's earthquake and angel are not included by the other writers. Both these images have ties to apocalyptic literature. An earthquake occurs twice in Matthew: at the death of Jesus (Matthew 27:52) and at the coming of the angel (Matthew 28:2). This recalls from the Old Testament the trembling of the earth in the presence of God (see Judges 5:4). It also suggests that the old age is being shaken up and the new age is being created. The angel, a manifestation of God, sits on the stone, symbolizing God conquering death through Jesus' resurrection. The angel's dress is similar to that of Jesus during the transfiguration (Matthew 17:2) and also echoes the apocalyptic imagery of Daniel 7:9. A similar description applied to God is also found in the Book of Revelation (1:14-16). The earthquake and the angel are reminders to Matthew's community that God's reign is here.

Exploring

If the resurrection accounts were concerned with historical accuracy, the listing of the women would have been consistent in all Gospel accounts. Mary Magdalene is mentioned in all three accounts (as well as in John's Gospel). The names of the other women, however, vary significantly. Matthew links three key events by mentioning women: The women saw Jesus die (Matthew 27:56); they saw him being placed in the tomb (Matthew 27:61); now they are the first witnesses to the resurrection. They return to the tomb not to anoint Jesus (this was done by the nameless woman of Matthew 26:6-13) but to inspect the tomb. More than likely, Matthew is following the Jewish custom for family and friends to watch the tomb for at least three days to verify that the person is dead. Their original intention (watching over a place of the dead) gives way to a new ministry—proclaiming that Jesus is alive. The women's reaction to what they experience is an example for all Christians: They obey the angel's command and become the first evangelizers, bringing the message even to the disciples.

Discovering

Matthew's Gospel ends with one of the most profound statements in Scripture—the commissioning of the apostles.

Read Matthew 28:16-20. In the space provided, write the key elements you discover in the passage.

Exploring

Compare your listing with mine.

- Eleven apostles are referred to, rather than twelve.
- The disciples are on the way to Galilee.
- The disciples are summoned to a mountain by Jesus.
- Jesus tells them that full authority has been given to him.
- He gives this full authority to the apostles.
- Jesus is with us always.

The reference to eleven rather than twelve apostles is a sad reminder of Judas' actions. The eleven are the nucleus for the new movement. They will spread the faith to all peoples. Their ministry begins in Galilee. Jerusalem will become in Matthew the symbol of death, while Galilee becomes the symbol of life. The life theme is heightened by the disciples being summoned to a mountain, which for Matthew has been the special place of God's revelation. The disciples respond by falling down in homage and adoration of Christ.

Jesus proclaims his full authority. The authority that was previously found in the Law is now found in the true Son of Man. In turn, he gives his authority to the Church to make disciples of all nations—Jews and Gentiles alike. People become disciples through Baptism, the public manifestation of faith in Christ. Through Baptism people join the Church and are ready to announce the Kingdom of God. All the sermons in Matthew's Gospel come to fruition through Baptism. The Kingdom is announced and the people are served. Jesus remains always in the Church; he is truly Emmanuel.

Looking Back

In Journey 18, you made the following discoveries:

- Comparing a Gospel account with the similar accounts in the other Gospels is a way to gain insight into the Gospel's message.
- The time of the resurrection links it to the creation story of Genesis 1.
- The message announced to those coming to the tomb is that of life and hope.
- Matthew includes earthquakes and angels in his account as a reminder of his apocalyptic themes.
- The commissioning of the apostles sums up the sermons of Matthew's Gospel.

Exploring Further

Jansen, John. *The Resurrection of Jesus Christ in New Testament Theology.* Philadelphia: The Westminster Press, 1980.

Annotated Bibliography

Apicella, Raymond. *Journeys Into Luke: 16 Lessons of Exploration and Discovery.* Cincinnati, Ohio: St. Anthony Messenger Press, 1992.

A companion piece to the manual on Matthew, the book captures Luke's timely message and vital vision of the Christian life and teaches us how to live our Christian faith in these uncertain and troubled times.

_____. *Journeys Into Mark: 16 Lessons of Exploration and Discovery.* Cincinnati, Ohio: St. Anthony Messenger Press, 1990.

A companion piece to the manual on Matthew, the book captures Mark's message for Christians by presenting Jesus as the suffering servant. Several "Journeys" provide further information on apocalyptic literature.

Babin, Pierre, with Mercedes Iannone. *The New Era in Religious Communication.* Minneapolis, Minn.: Fortress Press, 1991.

Although a nonbiblical resource, the book is an excellent text for those who want more information on symbolism. Babin challenges his readers to look to multimedia as a means of communicating the Christian message. The text would be of great interest for religious educators.

Beasley-Murray, G.R. *Jesus and the Kingdom of God.* Grand Rapids, Mich.: Wm. B. Eerdmans Publishing Company, 1986.

As the title suggests, Beasley-Murray offers a broad study of the Kingdom of God. Beginning with the Old Testament, he traces the understanding of the Kingdom of God for early Israel, the apocalyptic view of the Kingdom of God, and the teachings of Jesus and the Kingdom of God. The text is valuable for anyone who wants more information on this major theme in Matthew in particular and the New Testament in general.

Boadt, Lawrence. *Reading the Old Testament: An Introduction.* Mahwah, N.J.: Paulist Press, 1984.

Boadt provides a comprehensive overview of the Old Testament that is clear and carefully organized. Pertinent to our study of Matthew is the material on salvation history, prophetic writing and apocalyptic literature. Those with little or no background in the Old Testament will find this book helpful.

Boucher, Madeleine I. *The Parables*, New Testament Message, vol. 7. Collegeville, Minn.: Michael Glazier, Inc., 1983.

This volume is part of an entire commentary on the New Testament, which is an excellent supplementary guide for people who want additional information on any passage in the New Testament. Boucher divides her commentary into two parts: parables in general and a comparison of parables found within the Synoptic Gospels. Each section is an excellent resource for more information on parables and the role parables play in the New Testament.

Brown, Raymond E. *The Birth of the Messiah: A Commentary on the Infancy Narratives in the Gospels of Matthew and Luke*, rev. ed. New York: Doubleday, 1993.

Originally published in 1977, this updated edition is a complete commentary on the infancy narratives. Brown researched numerous studies on every aspect of the birth stories of Jesus. Along with language and exegetical background, he gives his own comments on the material. This work is considered the most comprehensive work on the birth stories.

_____. *The Death of the Messiah: A Commentary on the Passion Narratives in the Four Gospels.* New York: Doubleday, 1993.

With the same scholarship that he brought to his work on the birth stories, Brown presents a complete study of the passion narratives beginning with the Garden of Gethsemane and ending with the grave. Presented in two volumes, the commentary provides extensive background in language, customs and thought that have influenced biblical scholars in their study of the death of Jesus.

Brown, Raymond E., Joseph Fitzmyer, Roland Murphy, eds. *The New Jerome Biblical Commentary*, rev. ed. Englewood Cliffs, N.J.: Prentice Hall, 1990.

A major resource for biblical study, this commentary has been updated from the original 1969 edition to include advances in biblical studies over the past twenty years. The editors of this text are among the outstanding Catholic biblical scholars of our time. Of particular interest here is Benedict Viviano's excellent commentary on Matthew's Gospel.

Bullinger, E. W. *Number in Scripture.* Grand Rapids, Mich.: Kregel Publications, 1967.

The text is a handy resource to the importance of numbers for the biblical student. Bullinger offers the spiritual significance and the symbolical connotations of many of the numbers used repeatedly in Scripture.

Catholic Update. St. Anthony Messenger Press, Cincinnati, Ohio.

Published monthly, the periodical presents comprehensive treatments of various aspects of Church-related issues. Back issues are available. Of special interest to our study of Matthew are "What Is 'The Kingdom of God'?" by Richard McBrien (September 1980) and "Why the Infancy Narratives Were Written," by Raymond Brown (November 1986).

Collins, John J. *The Apocalyptic Imagination: An Introduction to the Jewish Matrix of Christianity.* New York: Crossroad, 1984.

The apocalyptic genre had a major influence on Matthew and his community. Collins provides excellent background to understanding this literary form and its influence on the biblical world.

Cunningham, Philip A. *Jesus and the Evangelists: The Ministry of Jesus in the Synoptic Gospels.* New York: Paulist Press, 1988.

Cunningham offers two major resources for our study: a section on Matthew's Jesus as the image of God and reflection questions at the conclusion of each chapter. His key idea is that Jesus is the incarnate wisdom of God and the Church is the incarnate wisdom of Jesus.

Ellis, Peter F. *Matthew: His Mind and Message*, 4th printing. Collegeville, Minn.: The Liturgical Press, 1985.

This book discusses the theological message that Matthew presents to his community. Of particular interest to our study is "Part Three: Theological Matthew," which provides detailed background into Matthew's understanding of Church, discipleship and Christology.

Flanagan, Neil. *Mark, Matthew, and Luke: A Guide to the Gospel Parallels.* Collegeville, Minn.: The Liturgical Press, 1978.

In this guide to Burton Throckmorton's text *Gospel Parallels*, Flanagan shares classroom notes from his courses. His section on Matthew's Gospel provides an excellent background to the five sermons in Matthew. Flanagan also provides material about the time, place and author of the Gospel, as well as information concerning the "Q" source.

Freed, Edwin D. *The New Testament: A Critical Introduction*, 2nd ed. Belmont, Calif.: Wadsworth Publishing Company, 1991.

Written as a textbook of biblical background, this book offers a good overview of Matthew's Gospel. Of special interest is the material on apocalyptic writing.

Harrington, Daniel J. *The Gospel of Matthew*, Sacra Pagina Series, vol. 1. Collegeville, Minn.: The Liturgical Press, 1991.

This commentary provides detailed background to and excellent understanding of the time, place and dating of Matthew's Gospel. Similar to other commentaries, it supplies information on the various themes presented within the Gospel.

Interpretation: A Journal of Bible and Theology. Jack Dean Kingsbury, ed. Union Theological Seminary, Richmond, Virginia.

The journal is published quarterly and contains excellent articles on one biblical theme per issue. Of interest to our study is Volume XLVII, Number 2, which deals with the reign of God and Volume XLVI, which covers Matthew's Gospel. Each issue contains major book reviews as well as short reviews and notices.

Jansen, John Frederick. *The Resurrection of Jesus Christ in New Testament Theology.* Philadelphia: The Westminster Press, 1980.

Jansen describes the significance of the Resurrection in terms of the whole New Testament rather than focusing on one particular account. He asks the question, "What does the Resurrection mean?" as a way of discovering its significance for the present age. For Jansen, the Resurrection is the key event of our past, present and future.

Jeremias, Joachim. *The Parables of Jesus.* New York: Scribner, 1963.

A general study of the parables of Jesus, this text is considered a classic in biblical studies. Although out of print, it should be available in the library. For the student interested in pursuing a more in-depth study of the biblical parables, Jeremias' book would be an excellent beginning and foundation.

Kingsbury, Jack Dean. *Matthew,* Proclamation Commentaries: The New Testament Witnesses for Preaching. Philadelphia: Fortress Press, 1977.

Although Kingsbury provides commentary to enhance biblical preaching, his text is also an excellent resource for those new to Scripture study. Kingsbury presents an in-depth study of Matthew's understanding of Church, God and Jesus.

Lachs, Samuel Tobias. *A Rabbinic Commentary of the New Testament: The Gospels of Matthew, Mark and Luke.* Hoboken, N.J.: Ktav Publishing House, Inc., 1987.

Lachs provides an extensive background to New Testament thought by examining its Jewish and Greek sources. His commentary lists numerous Old Testament passages, as well as ancient rabbinical writings, that have direct links to New Testament passages. Of special interest is his commentary on Pharisees and Sadducees.

McKenna, Megan. *Parables: The Arrows of God.* Maryknoll, N.Y.: Orbis Books, 1994.

McKenna brings her talents as storyteller and person of justice to her presentation on parables. Believing that parables cut through to the truth, she presents commentaries on the parables as well as provocative and challenging questions for everyday living.

Meier, John P. *Matthew,* New Testament Message, vol. 3. Collegeville, Minn.: Michael Glazier, Inc., 1980.

In this excellent commentary on Matthew's Gospel, Meier provides insight into many of the important passages of Matthew's Gospel. The entire commentary is a highly recommended supplement for anyone studying the Bible.

_____. *The Vision of Matthew: Christ, Church and Morality in the First Gospel.* New York: Paulist Press, 1979.

Meier provides an overall commentary on Matthew's Gospel as well as a section on each of Matthew's sermons. He is primarily concerned with demonstrating the important moral connection between Matthew's idea of Church and Jesus' teaching of the Kingdom.

Perkins, Pheme. *Hearing the Parables of Jesus.* New York: Paulist Press, 1981.

Perkins provides an excellent teaching on parables. She presents themes (e.g., "Ethics and the Parables") and the particular biblical parables that apply to the themes. Of special interest to our study are the five questions suggested as a way to examine the parables.

_____. *Reading the New Testament: An Introduction,* 2nd ed. Mahwah, N.J.: Paulist Press, 1988.

Perkins' second edition of her work, originally published in 1978, provides an excellent introduction to biblical study. Her first four chapters provide a clear understanding of biblical study, as well as the world and life of Jesus. A chapter on Matthew's Gospel contains a broad overview of some material presented in this manual.

Sanders, E.P. *Jesus and Judaism.* Philadelphia: Fortress Press, 1985.

Sanders attempts to answer questions about the relationship of Jewish Law and Jesus' ministry. He presents detailed arguments to demonstrate how Jesus fulfills the Jewish Law rather than breaking it.

Scripture from Scratch: A Popular Guide to Understanding the Bible. Elizabeth McNamer, Virginia Smith, Diane Houdek, eds. St. Anthony Messenger Press, Cincinnati, Ohio.

This monthly periodical highlights one topic on Scripture in each issue. Each issue includes sections on "Praying With Scripture," "Living With Scripture," "Talking About Scripture" and "Reading About Scripture." Of special interest is "Matthew's Gospel: A Community Effort" by John Wijngaards (January 1996).

Senior, Donald. *Invitation to Matthew: A Commentary on the Gospel of Matthew with Complete Text from The Jerusalem Bible.* New York: Doubleday, 1977.

The commentary provides a contemporary guide to Matthew's Gospel. Of particular interest are the study questions at the end of each chapter, which encourage the contemporary reader to apply the scriptural passages and themes to daily living.

Spivey, Robert and D. Moody Smith. *Anatomy of the New Testament: Its Structure and Meaning.* New York:

Macmillan, 1982.

This source is basically a textbook for college undergraduate courses on the Christian Scriptures. Although the text provides information on all of the Christian Scriptures, Chapter Three deals specifically with Matthew's Gospel. The text provides excellent background on Jesus as the Messiah as well as the world of the early Christian community.

The Bible Today: Scripture for Life and Ministry. Leslie Hoppe, ed. Collegeville, Minn.: The Liturgical Press.

A bimonthly periodical, each issue presents four or five topical articles on an aspect of Scripture. This journal is an excellent resource for the contemporary student of the Bible. Of special interest for our study is Volume 30, Number 1, on the end of the world. All issues contain book reviews of both Old Testament and New Testament publications.

Throckmorton, Burton, ed. *Gospel Parallels: A Synopsis of the First Three Gospels*, rev. ed. Nashville, Tenn.: Thomas Nelson, Inc., 1979.

This text is helpful in viewing the Synoptic writers in parallel columns. By reading a Gospel passage while looking at the parallel to other writers, the reader quickly notices "Q" material, shared material or individual sources. This text is a marvelous tool for beginning students of Scripture.